DEARLY BELOVED

By the same author: NORTH TO THE ORIENT · LISTEN! THE WIND
THE WAVE OF THE FUTURE · THE STEEP ASCENT · THE UNICORN
GIFT FROM THE SEA

ANNE MORROW LINDBERGH

DEARLY BELOVED

A Theme and Variations

A HELEN AND KURT WOLFF BOOK
HARCOURT, BRACE & WORLD, INC., NEW YORK

Grateful acknowledgment is made to Mrs. Norma Millay
Ellis for permisson to quote from Edna St. Vincent Millay's
"Prayer to Persephone," published by Harper and Broth-
ers, copyright 1921, 1949, by Edna St. Vincent Millay.

The excerpt from "Love and Marriage," music by James
Van Heusen, words by Sammy Cahn, copyright 1955 by
Maraville Music Corp., is used with permission.

⊮

CONTENTS

Before

Dearly beloved—late again!

Deborah pulled the tissue paper out of the sleeves of her new dress. Already three thirty and she wasn't yet dressed—for her own daughter's wedding. John would be furious. Such a punctual man, always irritated at her being late. Even after all these years of married life, he had never got used to it. And she never seemed to manage to leave enough time—even on Sally's wedding day.

Dearly beloved! Deborah had gone over the service so often that it kept running through her head, popping out all day like a mild swear-word in moments of distress.

Where had it gone to—the day? Breakfast. She could hardly remember back that far. She let Sally sleep, of course, her wedding morning. The other children straggled down late, rather out of sorts. Susie was teary and Ted had a nosebleed. Jake never turned up at all, because of the party last night. They were still sitting around the table when the florist's truck appeared, and the caterer's with the wedding cake.

And then everyone came at once: Henrietta to help in the kitchen—her own sister, after all, she didn't mind that so much. But some friends of Sally's with last-minute wedding presents, and one of the musicians to set up stands, and then—this was the moment John chose to get her in his study and ask if she had any idea what all this was going to cost? As if she could sit down and figure it out at that moment, with people running in and out and the telephone ringing.

Jake was supposed to answer it, but he had shut himself up on the third floor with his saxophone. She could hear him now over her head, dressing for his sister's wedding and taking time off to tune up on the wedding march. No, it wasn't the wedding march. She stopped halfway to the bureau and listened to the plaintive bleats of the saxophone, staggering down the scale with a kind of drunken despair. No, it was—for heaven's sake—Chopin's Funeral March! He must be mad—no, just adolescent.

Deborah jerked open the top drawer of her mother's old mahogany bureau, for a handkerchief.

I suppose he minds losing her, too, she reflected. Under all his guffaws and jokes, he was the closest to her. It was the first break in the family. Sally wouldn't belong to them any more. She would be Mark's—Mark's wife.

Oh, *Dearly beloved!* Sally, a wife; Mark, a husband. Deborah couldn't grasp it, couldn't even look at it. Her mind shied off like a skittish horse.

She shook the bureau drawer shut with some force. It always stuck in the spring. As far back as she could remember, it stuck in the "rose-cold" season, when she was a child and tugged at it ("Run, get me a hanky, dear, out of my top bureau drawer"). It was full of Mother's fine lawn handkerchiefs then, and white kid gloves and bits of lace collars, all in neat piles, smelling faintly of rose geranium.

If only Mother were here today. Not as she was now, of course, an invalid and unable to speak to them; but as she used to be, firm and positive. If Mother were here, Deborah thought, it would be different. She would still feel young, even though she was the mother of the bride; still feel there was a lot of life left after your daughter got married. Now, somehow, she felt on the edge of the grave. No—not quite; but at the top of a greased slide down. She wasn't ready for that downward coast, vaguely resentful, as if someone were pushing her off the ledge.

Was that John whistling from the door? You could count on John to be ready, at any rate. Had somebody come?

Deborah ran in her stocking feet to the window, and peered through the screen to the shimmering drive below. No, only the minister's car and Father's. It was surprisingly peaceful—quite an ordinary suburban June day outside, with a brown thrasher coolly repeating his phrases, twice over as usual, just as if there were all the time in the world.

"Be there in a minute, John," she shouted into the sunny stillness.

Why did the mother of the bride have to be at the door, anyway? There were a thousand other places she should be. In the living room, seeing that everything was ready. She could hear the muffled thuds below her, now. Someone still moving chairs about, or—that rolling sound— flower tubs, was it? And what was happening in the kitchen? A whiff of coffee floated up through the window. Were they all sitting around having a pre-wedding pick-up?

But Sally, that was really it—she should be with Sally. If she hurried (pinning her mother's amethyst brooch in the front of her dress) she could stop on the way down and look at the veil again. The bandeau was still heavy. Those two wings bent around—a little Valkyrian. She had started snipping at the feathers with nail scissors from Sally's dressing table—the only pair she could find. Where *were* all the other scissors? Taken to open wedding presents, probably, and not put back. So maddening to lose anything. You couldn't really rest—like a mosquito whining around your head at night—until you put your hand on it. It wasn't as though she were an untidy person, Deborah thought in irritation. They were all brought up to be tidy in her family. She never misplaced anything, normally.

But that room of Sally's—such a mess—you couldn't find a thing. Just like her room at college this first year. And Chrissie didn't help much as a roommate. How could they bear to sleep in it, those girls, or even thread their way across the debris at night? It didn't seem to bother them at all. Sal would rush right out and leave it like that, even today.

Well, *today*—Deborah hesitated—perhaps she could give it a once-over on her way down. No, there would be no time. Later, perhaps, after the wedding, after it was all over.

All ahead, now, like a big ski run. She felt as she did on top of the mountain, her knees trembling a little at the height, the distance to go. Such a long way and such a leap across unknown threats, before one reached safety and stillness at the bottom. Such an eternity before the end of this day.

Would she make it all right—get through without crying? It would be awful to break down in the middle, in front of everyone. Mother never would, or Grandma.

Deborah glanced up at the old portrait over the mantel. "A long lifetime of self-control," Mother had once boasted of Grandma. Erect, beautiful, but rather stern, Grandma looked, in her high boned collar. Deborah envied that erectness today. Not that she was ever *un*controlled, exactly. Never drank or anything. Not like Mark's father—at least, everyone *said* Stephen drank. Poor Frances, would she be able to control her husband, keep him sober this afternoon? There was the champagne, of course. John would have to watch it, though he himself never drank and really disapproved. No, he couldn't do it; it might upset him.

Father, then—Father could manage anything. He wasn't like any other man she'd met. So serene always, even today—even without Mother. How did he manage it? Was it something that came with age? Then it should be happening to her soon, "The Mother of the Bride." It sounded like a society column—"The Mother of the Bride." She wore lace usually, or something soft—gray chiffon, perhaps, flattering to the older woman.

Surely, she wasn't there *yet*?

Deborah peered into the mirror, daubing powder a little recklessly on her nose and under her eyes. Her hair was still brown, just a little gray at the parting. And her figure was fairly trim, after four children.

She drew herself up, pulling in her stomach as she rewound the sash around her waist, and looked at the dress so carefully chosen. Printed silk, scattered field flowers, a tidy all-over pattern on the disguise principle Mother taught her. It didn't show your figure. Not too bad, Deborah thought, though the skirt was still uncomfortably short. She could never look smart, no matter what she did. Not like Mark's mother. Frances would look like a fashion page, gray hair and all; maybe it was the make-up.

Deborah tightened her mouth to put on the lipstick. Would she be kissing people? Probably not. She had at Henrietta's wedding, of course, but that was a long time ago. Fifteen years, was it, that Henrietta and Don had been married? She had been the young matron of honor. She was the oldest then; Agnes had died. And Agnes's wedding—even further back, before her own. How beautiful Agnes had been, the only real beauty in the family— while she and Henrietta were just "nice fresh girls," Father used to say. But Agnes was beautiful—like Sally, a blonde Botticelli beauty, fragile like blackberry blossom or columbine.

Deborah bit her lip—the wedding bouquet, that was what bothered her. The white columbine looked droopy already. There wasn't room for it in the icebox, along with the champagne, and the wedding cake, and the sandwiches Sigrid had been making.

Was that the saxophone again? She must stop Jake before the guests arrived. What would they think, coming in the door, to hear Chopin's Funeral March? "The Wedding Guest here beat his breast," she remembered from Miss Finch's elocution classes, "For he heard the loud bassoon."

No—not the saxophone—the musicians. They were already in the living room, tuning up. She could hear the violin teetering for the right note. Was the music too sentimental? They really should have consulted Mark's Uncle Albert. He was the musician of the family, a real authority—people called him "The Maestro." Would he be peeved?

Well, it was too late now. "The Wedding Guest he beat his breast, Yet he cannot choose but hear—the Wedding Guest—"

But it was Sally's wedding, her daughter, Sally. Deborah drew herself up sharply. She shouldn't be reciting poetry or thinking about Albert's peeves or the crowded icebox. There was something else to think about. She couldn't seem to get to it. All those details, like a hedge of briers, kept her from the heart of it—what she was really feeling. As soon as she cut down one detail, another sprang up to take its place, another thorn pricking at her: the saxophone, the wedding veil, the lost scissors, the drooping columbine.

Almost as if she were trying *not* to think, holding off some realization, bartering for self-control. But the big things always caught up with you in the end. There came a moment when they broke through and you had to fight tears. She remembered from other occasions: Henrietta's wedding, Agnes's funeral.

A knock at the door, hesitating but solid, a child's knock. It was Susie; the boys would burst right in.

"Yes, dear?"

Susie looked very sweet, rather Kate Greenaway in that yellow smocking. After all, Deborah thought, she couldn't be *too* old, if she had a child of eight.

"Sally says please come right away and look at her bandeau."

Ah, Sally wanted her! Sally still wanted her—she must go.

Anyway, this room was in order; it calmed her to look

at it: her bed a cool cave, shadowed by its canopy; her books, solid to the ceiling, like an old stone wall buttressing the corner; her desk with its neat cubbyholes; her mantel with the honeysuckle and roses perfectly balanced at either end. And Grandma's portrait above—yes, she was in control now. The room held her, a still pool of composure and safety. How long until she would find its quiet haven again?

Out in the hall the house was no longer quiet: footsteps below and banging doors; voices from the pantry and a telephone ringing.

Deborah stopped at the open door of her daughter's room. Sally was standing with her back to her mother, facing the long bathroom mirror. Chrissie was on her knees, fluffing out Sally's petticoat, her own bridesmaid's dress billowing up from the floor.

"Sally!"

Sally turned now and stood looking at her mother. Stiff as a tulip, that tiny waist encased in ivory taffeta, smooth over the high bosom, with the skirt full as a ballerina's.

Swan Lake, thought Deborah, but she could say nothing. Sally's blonde head was erect under the feathered band; her face, grave but flushed. Her mother stared at her speechless.

She looks like a perfect stranger, thought Deborah, or— No, like Agnes, years ago. Still baby-faced though, the way she looked at eight, dressed up in her mother's clothes. Or was it the Snow Queen in the fairy tale?

There was a sudden explosion of gravel from the driveway, and John's whistle again, sharp and insistent.

The three women stopped, frozen for a moment of hesitation before action. Nothing but action after this moment, poised on the towering tip of a wave, about to fall into a thousand particles of turmoil: here, there, everywhere—scattered in different directions. But now, this second of still suspense, of withdrawal before the plunge. Wait—oh, wait!

"Debby!" John's firm shout from the doorway jolted them into action again.

"Oh, Sally!" Deborah went to her daughter, kissed her lightly on the forehead, and hesitated for a moment, looking urgently, almost pleading, into her wide eyes.

Wasn't there something she could say at this moment—mother to daughter—something real? Sally, too, seemed to be pleading, asking for some confirmation under her Snow Queen pose.

"Your father will be up—" Deborah blurted out in a rush. All she could say. The words for good-by never came at the right moment. Would there be another moment, perhaps—after the wedding? She always needed another moment. The real thing never got said.

After supper, maybe, she could slip away from the guests, as Sally was changing. On this small steppingstone she turned and hurried to the stairs. There were footsteps now on the gravel, and voices, and a car door banging sharply shut. Deborah clattered down the stairs on her high heels.

Dearly beloved, we are gathered together . . . "John—oh, John!"

In This Company

The big living room that afternoon shimmered with light and people and flowers: rambler-rose bushes in pots screening the long French windows; full-blooming peonies, lush and heavy-headed on tables, their blazing pinks and reds lighting the room, mirrored in the glazed blooms in chintz curtains and chair covers, in the red-coated portrait over the mantel, in a flowered dress here, or a rose-covered hat there, spreading a glow like firelight on people's faces, cheeks, lips. The aura of blooms was on everything. Above all, the flowers mirrored the occasion itself; their rosy flush, their early morning rained-on freshness; their exact moment of budding, bursting bloom, expanding, opening up, spilling over with wedding anticipation. *Here it is*, they seemed to beckon, *here is June; here is life, beauty, love!*

For whom did they bloom and beckon? The bridal pair? At the core of the drama, what could they see—to what be beckoned? For the outsiders, the onlookers, the guests, all this bloomed and beckoned. Wedding vibrations spilled over into the anticipatory hum of conversation, low laughs, and whispery greetings.

There's Deborah, the sweet thing. Mother of the bride, so young, too. And her sister, next to her. It seems only yesterday Henrietta and Don were getting married. Sally was the flower girl, remember? I can see her now—just can't believe she's the bride today. How time flies!

Old Mr. Gardiner's bearing up quite well considering—his wife's dying, you know. No change, I guess. It's a wonder they have the wedding at all. But young people today can't wait. What's the hurry? I always say you're married a long time.

The groom's mother looks nice, doesn't she? But why wear black to your son's wedding? Or navy, is it? Nice-looking, anyhow. I always say, if the groom has a nice mother—

But his father, you know—over there talking to Don—looks dissipated, too, don't you think? Handsome though, isn't he? Takes after his mother.

The old lady's on the sofa. Don't look now, but where did she get that hat? Unsuitable, I'd say, at her grandson's wedding. I may be old-fashioned but—

Sally's Aunt Harriet is quite a contrast, isn't she? Must be eighty, if she's a day. Never married—three times a bridesmaid, you know.

Who's the bridesmaid today—Chrissie? Over there flirting with the dark-haired boy. He must be the best man, came all the way from France to be in the wedding. So romantic, isn't it? There's something about weddings.

I don't see the father of the bride. Perhaps something's gone wrong. The groom's forgotten the ring, or— I went to a wedding once— No, my dear, just never appeared! We waited and waited. Such a strain on everyone, weddings, I always say.

Four o'clock, and the Maestro hadn't yet come. Deborah glanced anxiously at the roomful of guests. Everyone there, except Albert. They couldn't very well start without him—Mark's uncle, and such a figure, too. But how long could they wait? The minister had a train to catch and the musicians kept shifting their chairs about.

I suppose we could start the music, she thought, turning around for someone to ask. But what music? The Bach and Handel must be saved for the service. Anyway, you couldn't have anything too demanding. *Eine kleine Nachtmusik*, perhaps?

Ah, the music, the music had started! Conversation eased to a sigh, like an evening wind in the trees. Just a rustle of whispers remained. All the leaves now turned the same way, swept by this breeze of music. At last, the music.

It was beginning, then. The guests could stop talking, drop the cords of conversation—such a relief—the threads binding one person to another. They were through with the fixed pattern of dancing-school steps on a square foot of floor; forward, to the side, back; advancing nowhere, these tentative steps, since the steps they were waiting for, the only steps that mattered, led to the altar.

But now, with the music, the pattern was broken. The dancers were no longer interlocked. They could stop facing one another; let go hands, speech, eyes. They could sink into themselves, each person standing alone, steeped in the music, invisible in the music, free in the music.

It was not until the musicians had reached the end of the Mozart and had started "Sheep May Safely Graze" that a ripple of excitement, like a change of wind before storm, reached the room. The guests stirred uncomfortably, as if in sleep, noticing, then trying not to notice, the disturbance. When the muffled voices reached the landing, everyone knew who had arrived.

Must be the Maestro, seen him at concerts, of course. You'd recognize him anywhere with that shock of white hair. The Gallatin nose, too. Is that his third or fourth wife? My, my, some people never learn.

An unmistakable air of formality overtook the room, a crystallization where all had been fluid before. The country-house living room was solidifying into a formal hall—almost a church. The guests who, during the music, had half forgotten where, or even who, they were, now became conscious of their positions. Should they stand here or there? Where would the Maestro go? The bride's mother? This way and that, they peered awkwardly. Slowly the groups began to shift, lining up on both sides of the room, drawing back to leave an aisle for the bride and groom. Even the music, which had been light and charming, drew up sedately to a dirge's pace.

The Maestro, still coasting on the flurry of his entrance, proceeded with dignity to the sofa to greet his mother. Old Mr. Gardiner rose to give his place. He had done his duty, now; he could go to his own family, near Deborah or Henrietta, perhaps. There he would be free, at last, to think of his wife, ill at home but with him in spirit. Suzannah, he addressed her silently, it is beginning; our grandchild is about to be married.

The room, barely quiet again, suddenly resounded to a muffled chorus of footfalls. Mark and the minister—trying not to keep step like an operatic entrance, yet determined to get it over with—tramped down the hall steps and through the bare aisle left open between the two groups. They took their stand by the far window, studiously disregarding a roomful of guests furtively staring their way.

Look, the groom—the groom is there!

Mark! thought Frances, looking at her son's dark hair and ruddy cheek, half turned away from her. How handsome he is, how handsome. And she continued to look at him long after the rest of the company had faced toward the landing.

The music, muted now, was trailing out of reach like notes in a dream, the flute mountain-clear but far away. For the bride—Frances read it in the tightening of muscles on Mark's face—the bride was coming.

The Wedding March

The wedding march—there it was, ponderous as a plush carpet rolled out in front of them. Balanced on it, precariously as though treading a narrow path, came the bride on her father's arm; her veil, all honeysuckle and morning mist, barely stirred as it swept forward in little laps. Her father, rigidly staunch beside her, advanced in jerky strides. Eyes straight ahead, faces expressionless, the pair moved like sleepwalkers toward their destination.

"Here comes the bride." Everyone hummed it, kept tune to it, caught each footfall on thin-drawn breath. All action, drawn out to slow motion, toned down to a funeral dirge. Participants and onlookers alike were frozen in a spell imposed by the wedding march. Was it the pall of mortality itself: time passing; people aging; life sliding by? Every instant of daily life ticks mortality as irrevocably as this moment walking to the altar, but the tick falls unnoticed, like a dry leaf. When the wedding march sounds its resolute approach, the clock no longer ticks; it tolls the hour. Mortality echoes in everyone.

Everyone knows the ultimate destination of that solemn march up the aisle. Everyone paces it, drawn into its train, borne inescapably a little further along the way. A breath nearer than before; a step toward death; a pace to eternity.

No wonder mortal bearers of this destiny tremble under the burden, stiffen themselves to carry its weight, feel their small human forms inadequate to fill the great frame of the abstract. The figures in the aisle are no longer individuals; they symbolize the human race.

But the crowd of wedding guests could avoid thinking of the destination; they could concentrate on the couple starting down the road. This was easier. Fasten the attention on them; let the emotions run off there in little rivulets. "Here comes the bride." This was what they had come for and were waiting for—to focus like burning glasses on these two young people. On this wedding-cake couple, raised for a few seconds to a new elevation, they could lay the heavy burden of their dreams and memories.

Such a perfect couple! What a beautiful bride. Just radiant in her wedding dress. You can almost hear her breathe. Must be nervous, poor dear. Makes you want to cry. Looks like her mother —looks like her aunt— No, looks like her grandmother. Lovely, lovely! Just the most perfect bride. Isn't he a lucky man!

Now, they're almost to Mark. Poor boy, must be nervous. So handsome, too. Look at those shoulders. How good-looking! Better-looking than his father. Better-looking than his uncle. Better-looking than his grandfather. Always said he was the best-looking member of the family. Isn't she a lucky girl! So much in love. Aren't they the most perfect couple! Sssh—

The wedding march fumbled to a close, tiptoeing apologetically away. Silence roared back into the room, beat against eardrums. Only the flutter of paper as the musicians folded their scores on the stands, and a few suppressed coughs and whispers among the wedding guests.

You can hear a pin drop, can't you?

"Dearly beloved, we are gathered together . . ."

This was the gathering point. All the strands were drawn together at this moment, pulled taut, tied in a knot of supreme tension. This was the unbearable moment. One of those crossroads of life where the past and the future meet and fuse in one incandescent focus of the present, too much for the human crucible to bear. Moments like this demand a frame of formality, old and immutable as graven stone, beautiful and worn as stone, cold as stone. But even in stone the moment is overwhelming.

Through the cleft of the present rush the swollen streams of the past; a tidal wave, rising, surging, flooding the gap of the now. Will it break? Will it overrun the steep walls of the immediate? Not only time converges here, but human life and emotion and personality. The wasp-waisted instant is only one lens through which the rays converge. Each person is a lens for rays of past and future. Human genes, human hates, loves, and histories, human mistakes and hopes and memories, converge through each human frame at a wedding. Will it crack? Will it split—the frail lens of the individual?

In a blind instinct of self-preservation, some of the wedding party shield themselves against the intense rays of the moment. Too much to bear (for John, for Albert, for Henrietta, for Harriet). Too strong a current to let flow through them, exposing and shattering them—they, the strong, the armored, the invulnerable. Block it;

bandage the eyes; plug the ears; hold the heart. Let nothing seep in. Caulk up the cracks; bar the door; close the blinds. Batten down everything, and it will pass (for John, for Albert, for Henrietta, for Harriet). This is the unbearable moment, but it will pass. Thank God, it will pass, and everything will be the same again.

But for others (for Frances, for Don, for Deborah, for Theodore) life can never be refused. More courageous, more curious, or more greedy for life, no part of it can they bear to lose. Aware of its richness, its variety, they cannot close the eyes, plug the ears, or block the heart. In that moment of anesthesia some vision might flash never to be seen again (for Frances, for Don, for Deborah, for Theodore). Unbolt the door; fling out the windows; spread wide the arms. Let it come; let it flow; let it blaze. Let it pour through every vein. Let it flood the heart, immerse the body and soul. This is the moment, the unbearable moment. It will pass— Oh, too soon, it will pass. Listen to it; watch it; feel it—it will pass and nothing will ever be the same again.

Deborah

". . . in the sight of God, and in the face of this company . . ."

The minister's measured tones took over the wedding ceremony.

Thank goodness—Deborah breathed a sigh of relief—thank goodness the minister had taken charge. Now it would be all right. It was in his hands, now; his responsibility. He would carry it along. They knew how to handle these things, they were used to it—ministers, doctors. What a relief it was, with the children, when the doctor arrived at the door. You didn't have to make up your mind any more whether to give aspirin or whether to wait. They told you; they knew. She was never sure. Such a problem, always, to know what was right, when they were babies, or growing up. Even now—

But now it was out of her hands. Sally married— Oh dear—Sally's wedding. She couldn't believe it, couldn't even look at it. But here it was; here they were. In the sight of God, he said. In the face of this company. Sally was getting married.

But the worst was over, Deborah kept repeating. For her, anyway, the worst was over. That terrible moment when Sally came down the steps on John's arm. Everything rushed at her at once, too fast to see. All her life came back pell-mell—those pictures, one after another, till she didn't know which was which. Like a row of wedding pictures. Sally as a bride—or was it Agnes, her sister, Agnes, as a bride? No, Agnes was dead—not Agnes; Sally. The row of wedding pictures in the upstairs hall. Mother first, her own mother in a stiff white bustle—now dying, leaving her. Sally was leaving her, too. Agnes, Mother, Sally—Deborah didn't want to be left behind. But Sally wasn't dying; Sally was getting married. Sally in her wedding dress. Sally's picture would be in the upstairs hall, along with all the others. Next to her own wedding picture—Deborah could see herself as a bride—in that short skirt. A little girl, she was then; older than Sally, out of college but still hardly old enough to have a baby. Sally, her baby. Sally the day she was born. Sally as a bride.

Deborah's eyes had blurred with sudden tears at that point, couldn't see a thing. But it was over now, she repeated. She had looked away, at the flowers, at the mirror, at the minister's shining bald spot—anything to keep from crying. Now, everything was under control again. A smooth path. She knew where it led, what it said—

". . . *to join together this Man and this Woman* . . ."

Familiar steppingstones of the marriage service, one after another. She could follow them almost without looking, like the stones in her garden, smooth, well worn. Still, at each step she trembled a little, like John and Sally coming down the aisle. Each step was so tremendous. Would they make it, she had worried. Would John make it? Poor John!

John? Why poor John? Why did she worry about *him*? Her husband, John—the young, the strong, the invulnerable. But he looked so strange as the father of the bride, suddenly old and stiff—or terribly young and awkward, was it? A gawky boy, being brave and acting grown-up. But he *was* grown-up, not afraid of anything. Could it be—was he vulnerable, too? Sometimes shaken under that armor?

Everything was topsy-turvy today: John, an awkward boy; herself, a short-skirted teen-ager; Sally, a baby. Everything telescoped—birth, marriage, death—too fast to catch. She would like to stop it long enough to see clearly. Sometimes you caught a true glimpse of things, only for a second, a moment of vision. Most of the time life flickered on and off like a home movie; what you really wanted to see was just off the screen.

"*. . . in holy Matrimony; which is an honourable estate . . .*"

Sally as a bride—Sally as a newborn baby. That first moment when the nurse brought in the baby—she could see it now—the neat bundle of blankets, the tiny face, nested in the middle, startlingly alive. Smooth little face, fresh and new, yet strangely familiar. Grandma's nose, John's mouth, in miniature but quite clear, a family cameo.

With her head still floating in the vague blur of the white ceiling, Deborah remembered—rather like today— and her tired body painfully anchored in a hospital bed, she had drawn all her strength together, asked over and over, "A girl?" Incredible—"A girl?" Again and again that white-capped stranger had repeated the correct answer, the everyday, ordinary answer, "Yes, a lovely little girl."

A girl! She, this newborn baby daughter, would go through the same thing, Deborah remembered thinking. Had her mother felt the same way? Daughter—mother; mother—daughter. The cycle had been repeated; the cycle was starting again. This new life—what would it see? Where would it go? The future, at that moment, opened ahead of her, a long corridor of doors, dwindling in the distance, as far as she could see, until she couldn't focus on it any more. It blurred, like today. You couldn't look that far ahead, not for more than a second.

And then, when they brought in the baby the next time, she remembered, it was different. Not serene, not a cameo. Just a wriggling, screaming, red-faced infant, like all other infants—was it really hers?—making that curious rasping sound. Not like a baby at all, some kind of animal—a lamb, bleating, hungry for food, for milk. How sore her breasts were. She was pinned back to the bed, to earth again. The moment of vision was over; the struggle for existence had begun.

". . . *an honourable estate, instituted of God, signifying unto us* . . ."

Signifying *what*? wondered Deborah. What was Sally facing? The corridor of doors stretched ahead again, only you couldn't see behind them. What would Sally see, feel, cry over? Entering this honorable estate, commended of St. Paul. The service didn't say. Even St. Paul didn't say. Nobody told you: the comfort of sleeping with someone; the sudden terrors. The first quarrel she had wanted;

to run away. Luckily, she hadn't. "Not to be entered into unadvisedly or lightly," the Prayer Book said. Oh, no—

". . . *but reverently, discreetly, advisedly, soberly, and in the fear of God.*"

Yes, in fear and trembling she had entered marriage long ago. And here she was trembling again, for Sally. Much too young to get married. The innocent, the baby-faced—they looked serene and wise, but what did they know? Sheltered and coddled, wrapped up in blankets, they weren't ready to go out into the drudgery, the disappointment, the everydayness of life.

But what could you do? Protect them and hold them back? Keep them from living and growing?

You couldn't do that; you just had to send them out, blindly. Blind as a baby—closed-bud eyes. Closed gentians, someone had sent her when Sally was born, eyes tight-closed like a baby. Just the color of Sally's eyes, too, blue gentians. They should have been in the bride's bouquet. Too bad she hadn't thought of it. Closed gentians. It made you want to cry, a baby or a bride. She wanted to put her arms around Sally—or was it herself, the girl she had been as a bride? Comfort her, say to her, "My dear, my dear, it is not so dreadful here."

So dreadful? Deborah stopped short. What was so dreadful? Life? Marriage? What did she mean? Those lines, where did they come from? Out of her rag-bag mind, like an untidy bureau drawer, full of scraps and raveled ribbons.

Oh, she remembered now, a poem to Persephone ("Take her head upon your knee"), a plea for the queen of the underworld to comfort a newcomer ("She that was so proud and wild")—some girl who had died young. Agnes had died young. She was thinking of Agnes, not Sally, who was getting married. What was the rest of it? "Is a little lonely child, lost in Hell, Persephone."

Lost in hell? A wedding—marriage—hell? Deborah felt her face flush. She half glanced at the people around her. Had they guessed her thoughts?

The faces of the wedding guests were serene; their expressions rapt. No unruly thoughts; no untidy bureau drawers. They followed the service as if they had no doubts. Marriage was a holy estate. Beatific, nothing to be frightened of. Sally wasn't entering hell, but marriage, commended of St. Paul, a cause for rejoicing, honorable among all men. ("All, all honorable men," echoed in her mind.)

After all, hadn't *her* marriage been happy?

Of course, of course it had. Deborah was sure of that. A marvelously happy marriage—a wonderful husband, beautiful children, lovely home. Everyone said so. She was the perfect wife. Everyone said that, too. Even John. She seemed to satisfy *him*.

Wasn't that enough? What else could she want? But wasn't there something else, when she was young and in love like Sally? A glimpse, she remembered dimly—what was it? A kind of vividness—real life.

What was real life, anyway? Driving children to school, housework, picking up groceries, shopping, telephoning, helping with homework, passing sherry to guests before dinner: wasn't that real? No, it wasn't, Deborah decided, just scrips and scraps of other people's lives, like her bureau drawer, like her rag-bag mind—not *her* life at all.

Someday she would break through to her own life, Deborah resolved. Now that Sally was married, she would try. Stop running around; stop wasting time; stop being the perfect mother, the perfect wife. Then she would find her own life. Where? Not here, not now. Just around the corner, out of reach. In something else, outside of everyday life. In poetry, or music, maybe. She would commute to town and take courses. Look up a good teacher and study piano again. She always felt alive with music. Play the piano again, herself—that would be real life. Real life was ahead of her.

Or was it? Sometimes Deborah was not sure. Could it be—a tremor of suspicion broke over her, like waking up without enough covers at night—could real life possibly be not *ahead*, but somewhere *behind* her? In the past, in her youth? Was it back there at the altar, where Sally stood now?

"Into this holy estate these two persons present come now to be joined . . ."

Two people standing side by side, like herself and John, back in the wainscoted parlor of her old home, twenty-five years ago. Was it real then? In her knee-short wedding dress, John in his dark blue suit. It couldn't have been more unreal. She didn't remember a thing about it—just a rosy haze and dazzle of excitement.

And how good-looking John was. Still was, she thought, catching sight of his sharp profile next to Sally's; high cheekbones, chin jutting out, bony forehead. He hadn't changed much, just the hair graying and the skin a little lined, leathery.

One of those lean silent boys at college; quite a hero on the track team. Never talked much, rather unsociable, but everyone looked up to him. You could count on him to the last tight-mouthed breath, all the boys knew that. And the girls—his silence just made him more intriguing, sort of a challenge. They said he was a hermit, mysterious. Some kind of locked-up treasure in him, they imagined, had never been discovered. Each of them thought she alone had the key to the treasure. Except for her, actually.

She never dreamed he would ask her out. How flattered she had been, really awed, that first night. They were so sedate, too, sitting miles apart in the car, talking about the oddest things. Some sort of lecture, he had given her, on the effect of carbon monoxide in city streets. She'd been awfully impressed; but when the girls asked her, she really couldn't repeat it.

But so good-looking. The girls all leaned out the dorm windows when he came for her. Always on time, too, and brought her back at the dot of ten. (Such a dependable young man, Mother said. So intelligent and hard-working, Father said. Just what they'd always wanted.)

When he finally did propose, that night in the car, pulling her over awkwardly without a word, she was too overcome to resist. Nobody was very surprised. How could you refuse a man like that? Everything you wanted in a husband. "You could really trust John McNeil," everyone said. That was what she remembered most. She felt *safe* with John.

"If any man can show just cause . . ."

But that treasure they all imagined—that locked-up treasure—had she ever found the key?

What had she been looking for? She didn't really know; and things just came. Everything came so easily, so fast.

That first little house with the white picket fence made her feel married. Buying furniture with Father's check; the dining-room table—much too small, only room for six. "We'll never have more than four guests to dinner," she said to John, forgetting about children.

All those children, always a new one coming. Always sick, too—measles and mumps and whooping cough. She was forever carrying trays upstairs, and waking up at night to a crying child. Until the children finally got big enough so she could stop trembling for them—so big, they were bursting out of the old house, and then they had to move. What a spring that was, the year they moved—Jake with a broken arm; Susie, still a baby.

Moving was so depressing; clearing out, going through old things, throwing away a lifetime's accumulation. You looked back at your whole life, like today, and where had it gone? Into broken furniture, and boxes of old clothes, and thousands of little penciled lists of what to do, years of lists. She was still making them, still found them, in her new desk in this house.

Anyhow, it was a lovely house, this one. Everyone said so. Especially today. The roses looked beautiful in the window. The Maestro said so, and Beatrice and Spencer, too—her old friends. She hardly saw Beatrice any more, now she was married to Spencer—now she was happy. Did that make a difference? The years when Beatrice was unhappy and divorced, struggling to bring up Chrissie alone, they seemed to have more in common. Or maybe there just wasn't as much time now for friends alone. She and John had friends together, nice comfortable couples, pleasant evenings. She could never remember what they talked about—golf and politics. She left that to John. They always voted the straight Republican ticket, the stuff the country was built on, John said.

Yes, that was John, the stuff the country was built on. How firm a foundation, like the old hymn. But underneath the firm foundation, what was he feeling?

". . . *let him now speak, or else hereafter for ever hold his peace.*"

She never knew—that was it—she never, never knew. She didn't know him at all. Oh, of course, she *did*; it was only that she couldn't talk to him. She had another language: feelings, poetry, music; and she couldn't talk about carbon monoxide. He lectured; she listened. Married to a lecturer, a stranger, a foreigner?

No, foreigners weren't like that. Mark's friend, André, over there, for instance—pale face, dark eyes, sensitive mouth, rather good-looking. Whom did he remind her of? Prince André in *War and Peace*? Or some picture in a gallery? One of Manet's young men, perhaps; sad-eyed and elegant. That post card she had kept as a bookmark in her Tolstoy for years. Who's this? John had said when it fell out on the floor one night. She couldn't say my Prince André; it sounded so silly.

John thought Frenchmen a little silly, anyway—like that man on the boat, the year they went abroad— kissing her hand. How embarrassed she was the first time, her fingers open and stiff and hard, stuck out to shake hands like a man, instead of soft and smooth like a woman. She put cream on them for a month after that, and a little perfume.

André wouldn't kiss her hand—not today, not in this setting—but she put cream on anyway last night, after talking to him. A total stranger, just being polite. Foreigners were very polite, but you could talk to them. They understood things: a bride like a newborn baby— closed gentians. She could imagine talking to a French-man. Do you have gentians in your country? Would you show me some summer if . . . Madame, I would be so happy . . . and he would take me by the hand . . .

"I require and charge you both, as ye will answer at the dreadful day of judgment . . ."

Deborah shook herself. A cold draft, a chill, a rabbit running over her grave, Mother used to say. What would Mother say! Daydreaming—that Frenchman, what was his name? Prince André in *War and Peace*. She wasn't a young girl any longer, falling in love. This wasn't love, this kind of excitement.

Deborah drew herself up firmly, fastened her eyes on the bent heads of the wedding couple.

Not love, not marriage. Marriage was different: solid, real, lasting. This didn't last, wasn't solid. Just day-dreaming, imaginary conversations. But conversation it-self, the flash of understanding, talking the same language —wasn't that real? Communication with another person —wasn't it the realest thing in life?

". . . when the secrets of all hearts shall be disclosed . . ."

Suppose she had married a Frenchman—no, not a Frenchman—impossible. Not anyone she could think of, but someone else, someone she could talk to; not just about schools and money and plans for the summer. Someone to bring real things to, the day and all that happened in it; to unwind it slowly each night—the ribbon of the day; to share it. See, this is where I stumbled, and this is where I flew along—the smooth part—and this is where I got bored being a housewife, and this is where I got cross at Susie. And this is where I stopped still and listened to the thrush. Someone who cared.

John didn't care. The facts, of course, the problems, the decisions, she brought him every night. A colorless sort of ribbon *that* was. Not a ribbon at all, just a string, a grocery-store string with knots in it.

But the other things: what she felt, and saw, and heard. "How nice, dear," was all he said, over his paper. Even her triumphs.

And her worries, her failures—she never brought them any more. Just hid them, like a bad arithmetic paper in school. He couldn't bear her failures; he would pounce on them, like her old arithmetic teacher. "Look at this— See here— For God's sake!" He would nail her down, with the good strong nails of his logic. Bang, bang, bang, with the good hard hammer of his mind. Nailed to her faults forever. She couldn't move, couldn't walk away and leave them. Like a goose, nailed to the barn floor for *pâté de foie gras*. Nailed through a webbed foot, forced to go on gorging forever.

Deborah shifted her feet slightly in her high-heeled shoes. Much too tight, they'd have to be stretched again.

A goose—nailed down like a goose. How awful. In

France, they did it. So cruel. No, *not* a Frenchman. John was never cruel. Why not clip their wings instead? They couldn't fly away and they'd get almost as fat. Horrible, though. What was in the sandwiches today? She couldn't remember, but she mustn't eat them anyway. Deborah drew in her waist. Must be careful—middle-aged thickening—

"*. . . if either of you know any impediment . . .*"

Impediment? Not for her and John. Everything had gone smoothly. What was an impediment, anyhow? Speech impediment, people said sometimes. Not to be able to speak? Something blocked off—stuck? Other couples—did they talk? Couples in subways, couples in cars on Sunday, couples on park benches? No, they were lovers; they didn't have to talk. But married couples—was it impossible? Did other people share things? Talk the same language?

Deborah half turned to look around her. All the silent faces were slanted the same way, uplifted, as at a concert. Beatrice and Spencer stopped her glance, focused as though listening to the same music. Almost the same expression. Or did they really look alike, middle-aged and gray-haired? No, as if they were under a spell, all alone, no one else there. As if they were holding hands—

Oh, they were! Deborah stiffened and turned away. Not exactly holding hands, but touching each other's fingers, very lightly and inconspicuously, almost by chance. Deborah's own fingers were intertwined, twisting and tugging at her wedding ring. It wouldn't pull over the knuckle; too tight, swollen and calloused from that silly habit. She mustn't cry now; she couldn't go through *that* again. Look at the minister; listen to the minister.

"*For be ye well assured,*" the minister was saying.

Be ye well assured, she echoed to herself. This was better; this was what she needed.

"*. . . that if any persons are joined together otherwise than as God's Word doth allow, their marriage is not lawful.*"

The minister paused, a nominal pause only, to permit "any man" to "show just cause."

Just cause? Deborah held her breath. Silence towered in the room, asking to be toppled over. Would anyone ever dare speak up?

Oh yes. Father, she remembered, glancing his way— Father had once heard someone protest at this point. A rejected suitor, it was, at a wedding long ago. "I object," he had called out in the silence. It was an old family joke. "I wanted to marry Hannah myself." Would he remember?

Deborah studied her father's profile for some sign. His face was serious, unmoving, but under a bushy eyebrow she caught a twinkle of recognition, a quiver of compressed lip before he focused his gaze again discreetly ahead.

Oh, they were thinking of the same thing. Wonderful! Deborah felt tingling and warm, as though a screen had been removed between herself and a fire. They had a kind of understanding, like holding hands. Better than John or a Frenchman or anyone—to hold Father's hand. Nobody was quite like Father.

Had Mother felt this way? Father and Mother—had

they talked over things at night, brought each other the ribbon of the day? Had they understood each other?

Breakfasts in the old house, she remembered still. Mother at one end of the table, slitting open letters with a pearl-handled fruit knife. Father at the other end, with the newspaper held up in front of him, screening off the children on either side, but not screening off Mother. Glancing down the table at her, over the top of the newspaper, over the top of his half-moon spectacles. The pearl-handled knife and the half-moon spectacles flashed at each other above the children's heads. Glances, jokes, remarks, a secret language was exchanged up there on some level they couldn't reach. Neither she nor Agnes. They always felt left out; they couldn't catch the ball flying between their parents, to intercept it. Back and forth it went, over their heads, dazzling them as they watched, craning their necks to see, but never quite able to catch it, then—or ever.

Maybe, after Agnes's death—did something happen between Father and Mother then?—she was let into that private world. ("Deborah, my dear, your mother . . .") She, as the oldest now, had reached the upper level. Or perhaps since Mother's illness ("Deborah, dear heart . . .")—was he talking to her instead?

That night over the fire, that wonderful night, Father had opened up, talked to her as he never had before. About love, it was, too. So strange and unexpected. With Sally, it started, how much in love Sally was. And then Father had picked it up and launched a kind of sermon. To her or to himself? Or to that philosophy class he had always dreamed of having? She felt almost invisible; she didn't have to speak, just be quiet, listen, and look at the fire. And let the warmth flow over her, the warmth of fire, the warmth of words.

"You young people talk about love," he said, "as though it resided in an eye, or a foot—in a particular lift of a particular brow."

They were both looking at the fire. It was easier to talk looking into a fire; as if there were another person there, a third person.

"I used to feel that way, too, when I was young," he said. "Love was in the lift of a hand, and you wanted to touch that hand."

He got up at this point, and poked the fire vigorously, even impatiently.

"But it isn't the property of a hand or a foot," he insisted. "It doesn't dwell in the particular."

Was he impatient with her, she wondered?

"Love is a stream," he went on, "perhaps the stream of life." He stopped to stare, transfixed, at the blaze he had prodded into bloom.

"It is the stream of compassion which feeds the world." He was talking to the fire now, the third person listening.

"When you are in the stream and part of it," he said, "it feeds you, and everything you do and give is the stream flowing through you. You are a channel for love; you love, and people love you; it is all effortless."

Like the warmth of the fire, she thought, the warmth of light reflected back and forth between them.

"And when you are out of the stream," she broke the silence, "then where are you?" Would he let her into more of the mystery? "Are you always in it, Father?"

"Oh no," he shook his head wearily. "I've been out of it so much of the time—*most* of the time, I sometimes think. Then you're in a dry river bed and parched with thirst."

"Then what do you do?" Would she ever be in it, she wondered? Would she ever be near it? "How do you find it again?"

"I don't know," he said, shaking his head. "I wish I knew. I only know that it is the stream that matters. The hand, the eye, the shoulder—we cling to these. They express our longing for the stream—tributaries to it, perhaps. But it is the stream that matters," he said, "and not the tributaries."

The tributaries, that's where she was, Deborah thought, caught in the tributaries, wanting to hold his hand. Was it wrong, then?

"All my life I have been longing for the stream," he said, "only I didn't know it."

She too began to long for it, but if Father didn't know the way—

"In the beginning we are all pulled by the personal, the accidental," Father went on, "by the sound of a voice, the look of an eye. We think it resides in these; peace is in these."

He got up and stood by the fire, kicked a big log back with his foot, and watched the shower of sparks flare up, then wink out in darkness.

"An illusion," he said with finality. To himself now, not to her. He seemed to be getting further and further away. "We grope for the stream. Peace is in the stream."

"And what *is* the stream, Father?" Her voice went out to stop him, like a hand. If only he would go on. She felt on the edge of a great discovery, an illumination she would always connect with Father's voice, the fire—the stream.

"Who knows? Perhaps the stream is God," he said, answering her at last, "or perhaps God is the source of the stream. And women may be closer to it than men; at least, your mother—" He turned, then, abruptly away from the fire, as though he had been talking in his sleep.

"I must see if your mother is all right."

And there she was, left alone in the dry river bed, wondering.

"*Mark, wilt thou have this Woman to thy wedded wife* . . ."

The minister toppled over the tower of silence, and the room rang again to the good strong chords of the marriage vows.

Don

"Wilt thou love her, comfort her, honour, and keep her . . . and, forsaking all others . . ."

Damn lie, Don thought, *forsaking all others*. The phrase exploded in his head. Made him so mad it woke him up in his quiet corner. Had he sworn out loud? This was a wedding, after all, a family wedding. He belonged to the family, too, though only an uncle of the bride—uncle by marriage at that. Even so—couldn't swear at weddings. He looked around cautiously.

No, nobody stirred. Henrietta next to him hadn't twitched an eye—his good wife, and she'd have been the first to turn on him. They all would have turned on him—his in-laws, shocked, silent, but well behaved. Always well behaved, his proper in-laws, in their pressed pants, in their veily hats. How they'd stare!

What a story! *Bride's uncle goes berserk at society wedding.* Sounds well, that. *Social scandal, psychiatrist slips, swears at service.* Who's loony now?

Old story, old hat, old small-boy panic, wanting to shout in church. The minister was still droning on complacently. Hadn't he outgrown *that* yet? With his wife standing by his side and he a husband of fifteen years.

Married into that fine old Boston family, they said. Prominent psychiatrist. *Father was a dentist from the Midwest*, they said.

Father dug the dead pulp out of teeth; he dug it out of souls. The rubbish, the rot, he had to dig out. It was appalling, worse than teeth.

But that's why he went into psychiatry, to debunk people. Himself first—that was the hardest. Never quite rid himself of his small-town background, Bible Belt bringing-up. Damned persistent, that small-boy dream of fine families and ideal marriages. The one-and-only-girl-in-the-world myth.

Baloney!

That's why it made him so mad at weddings, the bunk people mouthed.

Forsaking all others—who could?

Not possible. Not for any normal person. Life just wasn't like that. The whole concept was against nature. Man was meant to reproduce, come hell or high water. No matter what—death, divorce, or desertion. Regardless. The urge went on. The glands didn't know the difference. They kept shoving you toward every attractive girl in sight. That was normal, not all this throwing yourself on the pyre when the mate died. Old Hindu taboo stuff, against the instincts.

Yet people went on promising to forsake all others and flaying themselves when they broke their promises. Or getting flayed—more like it—by their mates.

How they rattled the marriage vows in your face! Henrietta was always doing that—those terrible legal phrases.

What a rigid document. *To have and to hold*. No give to it, no mercy or joy. *Remain, continue, preserve*. Dead words.

No growth in them, no change. *Patience, faithfulness, peace.* Dead states. People got trapped in them. He knew; he saw it every day, patients trapped and beaten by those phrases. Couldn't live up to them; couldn't toss them over.

Look at that Carter woman—was that her name?— came in the office yesterday. That couple never should have married at all, and shouldn't have stuck together. Neither one would give in; lived on hate, those two, devoured each other. Immoral, he called it.

Fidelity, people said.

Immoral, it was. A death grapple.

His own father and mother were like that. He didn't realize it then, back in that little frame house, half dental office, half home. Did the divided house make it worse?

Just an accidental symbol, probably.

Father's office; Mother's parlor. Father's patients tramping on Mother's bulbs. Mother refusing to answer the doorbell. Always a tug-of-war. Didn't matter what it was: Father snapping up a window blind; Mother banging the oven door. Even the sounds and smells fought: red cabbage and iodoform; Father's drill and Mother's sewing machine—needling, needling, always needling.

What were they fighting about?

Damned if he knew. Everything: money, power, *him.* He used to think it was *his* fault and got out of the way.

Didn't help, though. Nothing helped, even when he ran away to Burny Jones, his only friend. Nobody really liked him in that town. Never knew why—

Early paranoia? Or just an only child? He used to think

people avoided him because his father hurt people, took it out on *him*.

Henrietta's family certainly looked good after that. No wonder he wanted to join it. No scrapping there. *Never a harsh word*, Henrietta always said.

Was that possible? Were any couples that happy? Old Theodore and his wife apparently were.

He glanced at the erect and rather portly figure of his father-in-law in front of him. There was something to the carriage of the old man, his bearing, the lift of his head.

Yes, there was strength there and sureness, too. Was it all a pose? The genteel tradition? New England sense of form or manners?

No, Mr. Gardiner and his wife had a good marriage. The girls all said so. That was the family legend. Some legend, too: *never a harsh word*. Something to live up to, *that*. Maybe just as hard as living down his family squabbles. Almost too good a picture, the old Gardiner marriage. Forsaking all others, cleaving to one only—there it was in front of them forever, the ideal marriage.

Something wrong with it, though; phony, he'd say. Otherwise Henrietta wouldn't have been the way she was. Not physical enough, was his guess. Not enough sex—unmentionable, sex. Everything physical was unmentionable, played down in that family. Things of the flesh didn't exist for the Gardiners. A wonder they married at all with their attitude, and didn't end up old maids like Aunt Harriet.

Manners and morals?
Swell.
Books and thoughts?
Fine.

Dreams and ideals?

Grand.

But never flesh and blood; never food or money.

Of course, they had plenty of the world's goods. That let them think it unimportant. Here it all was (Don sniffed the room): the pine paneling, the flowers, the good tweed coats, the soft carpets—gracious living and all that. It cost something, God knows.

The Gardiners must know it, too, but they never mentioned it. Money was too earthy. They were slightly ashamed of it, always, and ashamed of their bodies, of their hunger and needs, even their aches and pains. Unmentionable.

But this was what they lived on, these unmentionables: their well-fed upholstered bodies and pocketbooks, good solid seats they could rest on, glide along on with the greatest ease, and acting all the time as if there were nothing there, sitting on thin air.

It took a Boston background to do *that*—sit on air—like Henrietta in those Mexican outhouses. God, she looked funny, sitting on air—four to five inches off the seat—so she wouldn't pick up any horrible germs, she said. No use trying to dissuade her, poor girl; wouldn't listen to him. That was her training and she stuck to it. Certainly did. She could hold that position indefinitely.

Typical—funny he'd never thought of it before— typical Gardiner image. Never touched a toilet seat, the Gardiners. But toilet seats were there; so were money and bodies. Everyone ought to know that, even the people in this room.

What did they think—all these bozos in their best clothes, breathing down his neck, mouthing sancti-

monious phrases—what did they really think about
fidelity? Did they believe in it? Who was faithful in this
room? His wife, Henrietta?

If he stirred he would touch her dress. It quivered
lightly as she breathed. Out of the corner of his eye he
caught the glint of her sleeve, her bag crushed under her
arm, her hand clenching the Prayer Book.

He didn't have to look at her face—might catch her
eye, draw attention to him. Didn't have to look; he
knew. She was faithful, all right. Faithful because frigid.
Untempted. What was so virtuous about fidelity, with no
temptation?

But was that fair?

No, it wasn't, really. She was the loyal type, Henrietta,
always had been, back there when she married him.

God knows *why* she married him. Felt sorry for him,
probably. He was trying so hard to make her world; he
wanted to be a lawyer then, too. She'd have liked that,
more acceptable to the Gardiners than psychiatry.

Never would have done for him, though. He could
argue, but not in a box. Had to get out.

She stuck by him. Disapproved, but stuck by him, with
Gardiner dough, too, in the bad years.

Oh, he'd paid them back, all right. Yes, he'd paid them
back. He showed them he could make money, too.

It wasn't just the money, though. He owed her a lot, he
knew that. Henrietta had a kind of loyalty he didn't
possess.

But why were the loyal people always so rigid? Was
loyalty a substitute for love? Same substance; different
form. Frozen like ice.

What a difference, though! You couldn't drink ice, or

bathe in it. It didn't heal or refresh; it couldn't bring flowers to life or fertilize a garden.

What was it his mother used to say? "Snow is the poor man's fertilizer," over her bulbs outside the dental office. Funny connection. Snow was a blanket—protection.

But protection wasn't love, either. He'd had that as a child, plenty of it, from both of them. Mother and Father were always worrying over him. It was part of the tug-of-war, a kind of false coin they offered him. Solicitude, instead of love. Ersatz love, that's what it was. A blanket of solicitude—of snow.

Water, snow, ice; different kinds of love. Odd idea. What was steam, then?

Spiritual love, of course. Disembodied. You couldn't drink that, either, or bathe in it. But it had power; steam moved things—look at the mystics. He had never understood them; long ago gave up the idea of God, the all-powerful father. Hopeless search.

But spiritual love seemed to exist for some people. Don eyed his father-in-law's hair-striped coat in front of him. Perhaps for old Theodore spiritual love was enough. For the old, maybe; not for him.

He wanted things to flow. Love flowed; life flowed. That's what the rigid were afraid of—the fluidity of life. They had a fixed set of steps, instead. Not so much effort; easier to perform; it kept life nice and tidy.

But life was *untidy*, damn it. We pretended it wasn't. We kept weeding and straightening and laying lines. Life sprawled right over them.

You couldn't live in a jungle, of course, but well-groomed tennis courts were ridiculous, all weeded and taped down and rollered. They were always pushing rollers around—the rigid.

But every spring, dandelions break through the crust. Don took a deep breath. Wonderful life, pushing up endlessly through the surface! That's what saved things. Even in groups like this, there were dandelions. You wouldn't think so, with everybody flattened out to one dimension, but there were.

How about Deborah, now, in front of him, in that messy print dress? Any dandelions?

Nope—not a one. She was a faithful wife, all right.

So what? No man would think of touching her. Something about her, too delicate and cool, virginal—almost more virginal than the bride. If the bride *were* a virgin; you never knew these days. A nice handful, Sally; a bit on the skinny side for him, not enough to grab hold of.

That was the trouble with Debby. Not a bad figure, either, but she hid it in those sad-sack clothes. Ashamed of it, maybe, or frightened. A bit of Aunt Harriet in those girls. Henrietta was hopeless, but Deborah—had she withdrawn, or never advanced to being a real woman? It was a crime. Every attractive-to-man line—breast, hip, leg—covered up by a careful fold. Each wrinkle of cloth cried: Keep off the grass!

The groom's mother knew better. Frances showed everything she had in that dark dress: not an inch too much material, not ashamed of her hips. Was she a faithful wife? He didn't think so.

Not promiscuous, though—a certain tautness and meticulousness. But she'd learned to love with her body. At least one affair, he'd bet. Fallen into it in desperation, probably, with that neurotic husband.

Steve looked a bit hot and tense. Only a twitch of the eye, the jaw muscle stiffening now and then, showed he was making a great effort. He'd probably explode after it was over. She'd have a tough time tonight, poor girl. Hope the groom didn't take after his father.

How about Mark? Did any of them know anything about him? Met Sally on a ski weekend; celebrated family and all that; lived abroad. He bet Mark wasn't a virgin, in spite of that fine, clean look. The boy had a French friend; must know a thing or two. Those Europeans were pretty sophisticated.

Just as well to know something, Don thought. *He* didn't mind, though it would shock the pants off the Gardiners. He wished he'd had a few flings himself. A crime to be as young and clumsy as he was the first night. In that prissy New England inn. God, what a night!

Of course, you could play around *too* much, establish the wrong kind of pattern, like Albert over there. Had three wives already, not to speak of the others. Boy, were they naïve, these geniuses! Why did he go on *marrying* them? Hope Mark wouldn't take after *him*; harder on Sally than if he were a drunk. Nothing more suicidal than marrying a genius. Bluebeards, all of them, intentionally or unintentionally—musicians, writers, artists— no matter who they were, or how famous.

Look at the Maestro, now, brooding over the ceremony like a thunderhead. You couldn't help watching him. Something magnetic about him; his mass, his pose, vibrating for attention even in silence; his enormous vitality, even motionless. Geniuses were like storms or cyclones, pulling everything into their path, sticks and stones and dust. He used to see storms in the West like that. Nothing in their field of force could go against them. Everything had to rotate in the same direction—every dry leaf.

Every dried-up leaf of a wife. That's what she made him think of, Albert's wife. He couldn't even remember her name—so much like the last one. How soon they all grew alike: the same sucked-out-orange look; the fixed smile; the doe-eyed gaze of constant adoration. They must apply it like make-up each morning over their real faces, until they were gummed down for good. She hadn't been like that before. One of Albert's bright young pupils, quite a talent of her own once. Snuffed out, now— No, sucked into the tremendous updraft of his devouring personality, his genius.

Not her fault, poor girl. Or Albert's either, really.

How many times had Albert promised to forsake all others, to cleave to one only?

Impossible.

Geniuses just weren't meant for marriage, not in the usual sense. They should have another pattern; one adoring neophyte after another, a court of admirers, a swarm of satellites. They were meant to light a universe, not just one measly planet. They weren't like ordinary people.

But even ordinary people (Don turned his head away from Albert's rocklike profile), all these smooth-faced couples, profile against profile, like old pennies—how could they cleave to one only? If you were at all compli-cated—most people got more so as they went on—you were bound to be attracted in different directions. Different facets called for different responses, new friends, new relationships. For each new facet, perhaps, a new face—a new love?

But not a mate. Don, the professional, corrected himself. It didn't work out that way. You couldn't have a dozen wives, or more than one mother for your children. Impractical.

This was the regulation tennis court he had to play in. He knew where the lines were, and what was out of bounds.

Divorce?

Impossible. For him, at least. The pros and cons were all down in a ledger. He could read it off by rote. Bad for the children, divorce. Henrietta got by as a mother, provided a home for the children. For him—well, she kept the household going, kept things neat and tidy. Always well swept, his house. Henrietta certainly did her best. Good intentions—paved with good intentions and well swept, his hell.

But even so, he owed her something: security, social position, at least.

Besides, *he* needed the security, practically. Professionally too, as a base for his work.

How would it look if he made a flop of his home? A marriage counselor, too. And what a hullaballoo—divorce! Henrietta would fight it to the bitter end; he was sure of that. She would stand on her rights and hold to the letter of the law. Might win, too. Why do the righteous prosper? But then, what did they keep when they hung on like that—out of fear and possessiveness, out of hate, really? What was left in their hands at the end of that tug-of-war? An empty contract; empty of love, anyway.

But this was Henrietta's pattern; he knew he'd have to

face it. No use struggling. It took too much out of you—
time, life, money.

No. Albert's solution wasn't for him. One wife was
enough.

But how to make it work? What could he tell his
patients? Easy enough to give a flat dictum: sexual
harmony is the basis of good marriage. They all knew
that; taught it in nursery schools today. But how to
achieve it, or keep it? "Doctor, is it possible to have a
permanently successful physical relation with your wife?"
Earnest young man, wanted an answer. What could he
say?

It always stumped him, that question. Couldn't say *yes*
or *no*. Only *maybe*. But they always asked *how*. *How* to keep
a good sex relationship in marriage? How the hell?

He didn't know. He tried to give the young ones tips,
but the middle-aged . . . It would be easier to run a
column or write a marriage manual. You wouldn't have
to look at their tired faces, and listen to their stories, all
alike.

Marriage was so overlaid with executive details, the
business of running a home and family together. *Couldn't
you go off with your husband on one of his business trips, Mrs.
Carter?* And those endless problems of money and household repairs and in-laws getting sick. *Do you have to discuss
these at night, Mrs. Clark?* The children's teeth needed
straightening and the adolescents had allergies and the
teen-agers wanted strapless formals. "But, Doctor, the
only time I get to ask my husband these things is in bed."

Didn't he know! Henrietta was always nabbing him in
bed. They needed a new stove. Should they go out to
dinner next Tuesday or have the Dohickles here?

How could two human bodies meet each other passionately under the trappings of household details? Women were the worst; they carried it around all day—just couldn't take it off at night.

There wasn't any answer.

It was inevitable, after a while you looked for the new love, the fresh relationship, the warm body you met just as a body. The French were right about it: separate love and marriage. No associations; no baggage of pressures and duties. That girl in Miami—she didn't ask him questions. Just a sun-tanned body under your hands. You lost yourself; you felt alive. Thirsty, you drank, came away refreshed. Was it wrong?

Wrong. The uplifted faces in the room said *wrong*. The Prayer Book squeezed under Henrietta's arm said *wrong*, *wrong*.

Bunk, superego.

His guilt had gone long ago, analyzed away, dimmed under his many affairs—if you could call them that. It was easy, had become easy—but somehow less satisfying. The guilt had gone but, he had to admit, some of the glamour had gone, too.

Well, he was older, now—practically a great-uncle, with Sally getting married. It put him in another generation. How old he must look to them! Couldn't expect the same thing any more. Respect, that was what he would get now. Gratitude—transference.

Okay, he could help people, keep them from making mistakes. But how? Destroy the myths? The romantic myth: *There's a boy for every girl in the world*?

American sentimentality.

The fidelity myth: religion and all that?

An enormous conspiracy to control people, hold on to their strongest urge.

The monogamy myth?

A convenient traffic system of society to keep things tidy.

Suppose you took the whole bundle and baggage of it, heaved it up, and threw it overboard? Suppose you took sex as you wanted—as he had—like food or drink? No guilt attached, no fear. Did that fix it up?

It wasn't wrong but—he had an arid feeling in his throat at this point, as if he'd been drinking soda pop instead of water—was it quite right?

Here's where he gagged. Was this the solution? Was it satisfying? Did it quench thirst?

He was never sure.

It wasn't just a matter of physical hunger for pleasure and escape. You wanted love as well as sex. It wasn't as simple as the novels made it. You didn't just want to be loved by the perfect partner at a moment of perfection; on an isolated peak outside of daily life; in an air-conditioned room in a hotel. That wasn't enough.

You wanted to be loved in the midst of life, past your prime, paunchy and gray and tired, even discouraged and cross—in all your imperfections. You wanted to be forgiven your weaknesses, to be loved, in spite of them, for better or for worse.

That *was*, when you came down to it, what you wanted: to be loved "for better for worse, for richer for poorer, in sickness and in health." That was what it meant, what everyone wanted. He had wanted it, too, believed in it, once. He picked a lemon, that's all. *Why did I pick a lemon in the garden of love, where they say only peaches grow?*

Suppose he'd picked a peach, would it have been any different? Lots of peaches around. Could you promise to love a peach? Henrietta was a peach back there, pretty and pink and carefully raised.

But could you promise to love at all? "To have and to hold"—perhaps. "To honor and to cherish"—perhaps. But to *love*? That was even harder than promising to be faithful. He had promised to love Henrietta, fifteen years ago. She had promised to love him. Neither of them kept it, or even began to. Never loved each other at all, incapable of it, even at the start. Had he ever really been capable of loving anyone? Was he now?

There was no answer in the hushed room, only two other people promising to love each other forever.

Love, love, love, Don fumed silently. Why do we mouth that word day and night? In churches and books and movies; in living rooms like this, and in subway trains, to advertise lipsticks and brassières and chowders. What did it mean, anyhow?

An appetite, only. Sex was an appetite, obviously.

But love was a gift, like any creative gift, not handed out to all of us, or all of the time. You couldn't feel it for everyone, for your enemy or your neighbor, as the Bible said, or even for your own family. Least of all, your own family.

But in his work, now—

Music! They were interrupting the service with music.

What was it? Clear, limpid, drops of water, a spring bubbling up through the clay. He could put his face to it, drink it, revive. Everything smoothed out, like sex, like love. Didn't have to judge, didn't have to resist, just move along with it. Just listen. Only one voice to listen to—was it that?

No, lots of voices, hard to listen to, really, like listening to his patients, sometimes complicated. The voices flowed; he followed; the melody climbing up and down, the deep chords pacing underneath; then the phrase repeating in a new place. Exciting to keep track of it, not stopping it, letting it flow. Just listening, attentive, open— like love.

It *was* love, maybe, a form of love—what he felt, what he did, as a doctor: focusing on the other person, his needs, his hurts, his pressures; without judgment, or preconception, or resistance—a kind of open awareness.

You could cultivate this kind of love, practice it, even. He was learning; he couldn't always do it, sometimes it didn't work. But when it *did*— Oh, when it did, he lost himself; patients found themselves, loosened up, freed. Something happened—healing, to them and to him. Something flowered from his listening.

Love? Simpler, humbler, not what most people called it; but maybe it was what Christ meant. "Love one another," he said. Maybe he meant just this—openness, awareness, lack of judgment—and they'd got it wrong from the beginning, nailed it in a frame, nailed it on a crucifix. And Christ had meant: Listen to one another, listen to your enemy, listen to your neighbor, listen to your children.

Listen to your children— Did he?

Some, not much, not enough. Too damned busy; left it to Henrietta. Did he ever listen to *her*?

No, not if he could help it—not if he could possibly avoid it. He plugged up his ears, blocked himself off. Too busy to listen. Too tired. Had to pull down the blind, he couldn't take it: her fears, her jealousies, her compulsiveness. He knew about them, of course, heard it all long ago: shy as a child, jealous of her older sisters, never able to compete; got their hand-me-down clothes and beaux.

Poor Henrietta, her long struggle for attention still going on. She was always trying to do right and keep busy like Aunt Harriet in front of him. Stiff as a ramrod, that old girl; you'd never get her on a couch. But she'd never break down, either. That generation had their code and it never faltered. Keep busy; do good. Puritan bringing-up. Be a good girl.

Good girl, Henrietta; never happy. He hadn't helped much.

No psychiatrist could treat his own wife. He knew he couldn't cure her; couldn't even *love* her.

But couldn't he listen—couldn't he sometimes *listen* to her?

He didn't listen. That was a sin, all right, by his standards. More of a sin than infidelity. A sin against what he believed in, his particular gift, his creative faculty. A sin against the Holy Ghost—that was it—the spark of God in him, who tried to forgive people their debts, to deliver them from evil, to keep their fears from having dominion over them.

The Lord's Prayer! My God; soon they'd have to wake up and go back to life. Henrietta was shutting the Prayer Book, mouthing the phrases with closed eyes. So nice and quiet she'd been all this time. Soon she'd start to talk.

Damn it, if only she wouldn't talk so much. Oh, God— if only she would be quiet, *then* he could listen to her!

Aunt Harriet

". . . in holy Matrimony . . . instituted of God, signifying unto us . . ."

Aunt Harriet's white head was bowed during the opening lines of the wedding service. How many times she had heard these words. Three generations of weddings she had witnessed in her family. It took her back a long way.

She had seen all the others marry. Her brother, Tim—so handsome he'd been, and thrown himself away on that silly woman. Why men fell for that sort of thing she could never see. And then her sister, Suzannah—the flower of the family, everyone said. How beautiful she had been on her wedding day in her stylish dress, with the pinched waist and bustle. The high crown of her piled-up hair made her look taller than Theodore that afternoon, she remembered. And then Suzannah's children: the beautiful Agnes—too beautiful to remain in this world; and after her, Deborah and Henrietta. She had watched them all go down the aisle.

Signifying unto us—she ought to know what marriage signified, even though she herself had never married. People laughed at old maids and their opinions, but she'd observed a great deal from the side lines. Precious little had escaped her. Marriage, from what she'd observed, was for children. Everything else, in the long run, vanished away: good looks, physical attraction, all the superficial things. Man was cut down like a flower, but the shoots remained. As you grew older, you realized it more; the life force, the sap, was not in the old roots but in the shoots. One lived for the shoots.

"... *to live together after God's ordinance* ... *in the holy estate of Matrimony* ..."

The Prayer Book said it best in that paragraph usually omitted from the service nowadays. What a commentary on modern marriage to leave out the most important part. Holy matrimony was for the gift and heritage of children. She hoped someone had instructed this young couple properly. It seemed out of place for her to be giving advice, at her age, and an old maid at that.

Not that she never had a chance. She was no beauty like Suzannah, but she'd had some looks in her day. There was the boy next door. Father didn't think the family was up to their standards. And he was right, too, now she looked back on it. That young man's progeny, when he did get married, turned out to be brats, as she recalled. It seemed a long time ago; she couldn't imagine why she'd been attracted to him. Something just gets into the blood at eighteen. And there was that friend of Tim's, but not a patch on Tim. How could you take anything second-best when you had such a brother? And then that old widower Suzannah wanted her to marry, not so many years ago. Ridiculous of Suzannah, feeling sorry for her, saying she was living only half a life and would face a lonely old age.

Half a life!—when she'd been a teacher for thirty years,

and always lived just the way she wanted. Sometimes, it seemed to her, married people lived half-lives; having to compromise on every point, waiting on the other person's pleasure, scared to death of a quarrel or a complaint. As for being lonely, if you kept busy and active you were never lonely. There were plenty of people around. Maybe you didn't have love in one big chunk of gold, the way the married had—or said they had. She wondered sometimes, looking around her. But you had it in little pieces all the time. It was still gold; small change perhaps, but all gold, scattered through her life, in her friends, her pupils, her nieces and nephews.

Now her grandnieces and nephews, one of them on either side of her today—very well behaved, Harriet was glad to note, glancing sideways at their upturned faces. Perhaps they were a bit awed by the churchly atmosphere of the transformed living room. Sheila was usually good, and even Syd wasn't shuffling his black patent-leather pumps, as he often did at church. She was free to watch the wedding couple and listen to those solemn words:

"*Sally, wilt thou have this Man . . .*"

Dear Sally and her young man. How she had watched and prayed for them, and now they were taking their marriage vows. She was thankful to be here as a witness— in some measure a witness for Suzannah, who was slipping away from them, with her first grandchild, Sally, bending her head under the veil.

Why, the child *did* take after Suzannah at that. Harriet adjusted her glasses to get a better look. Theodore was right, and she'd never seen the likeness before. But today,

under the veil, Sally was the living image of her grandmother. Something about the profile. There it was again,
the New England heritage.

These two young people were certainly carrying on a
heritage, whether they knew it or not—a good one, too.
Harriet straightened her already erect spine at the
thought of the generations of New England forebears behind her grandniece. The names she had heard from her
mother and grandmother: the Obadiahs and Timothys,
the Sarahs and Prues, from stony New England pastures,
or little towns with big elm-covered greens that sheltered
the cattle at night, and white clapboard churches with
cold hard pews.

"Lord, thou hast been our refuge from one generation
to another." Generation after generation, going back to
the rough voyages from England, the long winters, the
children who died, all recorded in the family Bible.
Teachers and preachers, doctors and ship captains.
Grandfather had been a preacher; Father, a teacher. It
was in her bones—a goodly heritage.

And Theodore's family—Harriet relaxed her grip on
the Prayer Book slightly, as she glanced at her brother-
in-law's gray head in front of her—quite acceptable, too,
though perhaps not up to theirs. Not pure English; some
odd German or Dutch strain. He was a little heavy and
abstruse in his thinking, Harriet felt, and always made her
sound literal. Still, he had been a very satisfactory
husband for Suzannah; she had held her own with that
Dutch background. They had character in their family.
And Theodore, she had to admit, had been a good father,
too. The girls had married fine upstanding men—especially Deborah.

"Who giveth this Woman to be married to this Man?"

And here was Deborah's young bridegroom—it didn't seem possible—gray-haired himself, now, giving his daughter away in marriage. A fine young man, still, John McNeil. All you had to do was to look at him to know his background. Decent Scotch Presbyterian. He knew the difference between right and wrong, and taught it to his children. Too strict, sometimes, Deborah complained, but wasn't he right? Deborah was inclined to be namby-pamby with her children—with her husband, too. What was it about marriage that cowed people, made wives unable to speak their minds? She couldn't imagine not speaking her mind to anyone. She had been brought up strictly, too, in the good old-fashioned way—she and Suzannah—"in thy faith and fear."

And the fear was necessary, too, no matter what the psychologists said. Don, no doubt, would disagree. Wasn't he standing right behind her today? Harriet had an uncomfortable impression that she could feel Don's sharp eyes boring right through her back. Silly notion, that; he was most agreeable, though if she were Henrietta she would keep him more in hand. All this running around—was it really necessary? Of course he was a very clever young man, Don.

But somehow, this psychology talk—how could it be right? So much emphasis on the self: self-analysis, self-expression, self-fulfillment. It didn't make sense. All the wise men and the Bible pointed to *loss* of self as the road to wisdom. Even William James—and he was modern enough—said, "The self is what I hate most." If you had to talk about self, self-control and self-sacrifice were the things to stress. And this nonsense about inhibitions and frustrations—if you kept busy and active, you didn't have time to be frustrated, and you were happy enough, too. Though happiness certainly wasn't the point of life.

The point of life, Harriet had grown to feel, was finding the task one was meant to do. "Do ye next thing," as she had been taught as a child. One had to justify one's existence in some way, be of service to others, as she had tried to be—after Suzannah's illness especially—with her grandnieces and nephews. She had given them their Bibles and taught them their prayers.

"Our Father, who art in heaven, Hallowed be thy Name."

Harriet joined in the uneven mumble of voices repeating the Lord's Prayer. A comfortable feeling, almost like getting into bed, to sink into this familiar chant, to feel oneself part of this familiar group, all united by the old prayer. Even the children at her side were part of it, speaking up clearly the words she had taught them. Almost too clearly, wasn't it? She took a sharp look on each side of her. Some kind of contest was going on there. She could handle it all right, as long as she was between them. They couldn't very well fight across her. How it took her back to her own childhood: those strained undercover battles between herself and Tim at family prayers, all kneeling down by the horsehair sofa, knees and elbows silently digging in below closed eyes and folded hands.

But on the whole, children were good if they had good stuff in them and were trained properly. If they weren't the right stuff, there wasn't much you could do about it. In a family like this one, there wasn't any question. She had watched children come to Suzannah, and then to Suzannah's children. None of her own; but spinsters could appreciate children better than parents, she sometimes thought. Children were a gift from God. She never ceased to reverence the new world created before her eyes; brand-new, yet with those strange reminders of the past. Sally, there, like her grandmother. The wellspring of new life; and the immutability of heritage.

The heritage was pretty much overlooked today, Harriet felt. Who ever talked about heredity, discussing marriage? It was considered bad taste. People paid enough attention to breeding their dogs and horses. Only human beings, it seemed, were too high and mighty to be well-bred. Perfect nonsense, to her way of thinking. At least in her day, good breeding was not bad taste; parents considered the families their children married into. Hadn't her own father saved her from a bad match?

The Gallatins, now, who had considered that family? Harriet glanced across at the other side of the room. There were just as many ancestors behind Mark, it occurred to her with an unpleasant shock. What were they like? No way of knowing—that was the trouble.

To be sure, the Gardiner stock was strong enough to outweigh any lapses on the Gallatin side, but just the same it made her uncomfortable to look at that row of faces: their sleek well-dressed forms, their elegant profiles, all turned one way. Albert had his head in the air, as if he were posing for a camera. The grandmother, too, was old enough to know better, with that hat. And Mark's father, good-looking, but milksoppy—though not from milk, she'd heard.

Stagy, Harriet decided, or at least, Continental. Not a

compliment in her code. It suggested perfume and light wines—perhaps even incense? Something soft, at any rate. She liked to see a straight stick in people.

Mark had one, though; he must have got it from somewhere. His grandfather, perhaps? Or his mother? Frances looked sturdy enough. But if she were a regular woman, why did she have only two children, Mark and that buxom girl? Something Continental about that, too—a little effete. The old New England families were generous.

Come to think of it, there were only two children out of that whole side of the room to carry on the Gallatin name. What a burden for Mark! His Uncle Albert had no children, although he'd been three times to the altar. Harriet shook her head imperceptibly. "Whom God hath joined together . . ." Three times and no child. Theodore might say Albert had the children of his genius, his music—even his pupils. But soul mates were silly, Harriet thought, and brain children simply did not count. At least, not on earth. In heaven, maybe. On earth, what counted was—

"*O Almighty God, Creator of mankind . . .*"

Here it was, at last, the prayer she was waiting for. Not left out after all. Harriet sighed with relief.

"*Bestow upon these thy servants . . . the gift and heritage of children . . .*"

Now she could relax. This blessing, she was sure, would wipe out any Gallatin weakness.

"*. . . and grant that they may see their children . . .*"

But she—Harriet stopped short in the midst of her favorite prayer—would *she* see their children? The children from this new marriage? Great-grandchildren, or rather, great-grandnephews and nieces. Would she be able to teach them? Would she even see them?

Harriet took stock abruptly. She had had that little heart trouble last year. The doctors said it wasn't serious, just a warning; but one never knew. Seventy-nine, eighty, eighty-one, she began to count. "Lord, let me know mine end," she breathed, "and the number of my days, . . . how long I have to live—"

Not that she felt old; she had all her faculties and she could still catch a child scrambling under a sofa. But she was going on seventy-nine. Father died at eighty; Mother, at eighty-five. One never knew. Would she even be here next year? Would she still be of this goodly company? Would she be in this gracious room? So dear and home-like, so much a part of her; this was where she belonged.

She looked around at the familiar walls; the books, many of which had been her father's; the furniture, some of which had been in the old home on Center Street; the octagonal table, pushed now to the rear of the room. That narrow gilt mirror in the corner—it looked so small in here—had been their hall mirror.

Yes, this was certainly where she belonged. And those familiar faces: Deborah and John, Henrietta and Don, and all the grandchildren, so carelessly accepting of her presence here; as if she would be here forever, a permanent fixture, like the old mirror in the corner—when, really, she was hanging on in the most precarious fashion, a dry oak leaf about to fall from the branch.

"A sojourner," Harriet repeated silently, "as all my fathers were."

And yet, how could one expect the young to understand? That pretty girl over there in the green dress, Sally's friend, Chrissie, making eyes at the French boy. They only thought of themselves and their young men. It was natural enough. Even Deborah and Henrietta, with their busy lives—how could they keep it in mind that she might easily not be of their company next year? Why, she could hardly keep it in mind herself, or even believe it. Unthinkable, but she might not be here next year.

And death itself—at least the contemplation of her own death was always the same. Quite unlike thinking of anyone else's death, her mother's or father's, or even Suzannah's. One had been near it often enough; it was quite familiar at her age. The veil between the two worlds became very thin. "In the midst of life we are in death."

But somehow the contemplation of one's own death was different—almost a kind of dying. There was first a feeling of panic, a roaring in the ears, like drowning. And then one passed over to the other side, the spiritual side; and there she felt secure, in God's hands.

"He will lift up mine head"—a hand under her chin, she imagined, like her father teaching her to swim—"and lead me into still waters, to the green pastures on the other side." It was always like this, like crossing a river, each time she thought of her own death. There was the moment of drowning—and then the other shore, like Pilgrim's Progress.

Then she would imagine—like daydreams in her youth—she would be of that other company, that fellowship of saints. Her father and mother, Suzannah, perhaps? Suzannah might get there first, in spite of her being younger. Her brother, Tim. It would be good to see Tim, without that silly wife. Surely one wasn't still tied to spouses in heaven? After all, Christ said there was no giving or taking in marriage in heaven.

Heaven was difficult to imagine. The Sunday-school pictures had faded away, and the phrases in the Prayer Book were rather dim on this point: resting from their labors, watching from above. Resting? Watching? Watching only—unable to act? Unable to help, to lift a hand or tie a shoe? Harriet's New England energy rebelled at the thought.

But then, any more vivid picture of life beyond the grave was just as bad. Any of that truck with Ouija boards or mediums or Indian reincarnations was downright offensive to her, like seeing the good clean light of day through cheap stained-glass windows in lavatories.

Not for her, any of that. Theodore might call her literal but she wasn't going to be like the man in the Bible saying, "How are the dead raised up? and with what body do they come?" One must not try to see too clearly. Heaven, she was sure, couldn't be inactive, world without end. There would be some life of service, some place for her. "In my Father's house there are many mansions." Surely the dead also helped; she must wait until she was of their company.

All one knew about death was that it was coming. This year? Next year? One didn't know. One only knew that it was coming. She was still on her pilgrimage; she must walk by faith. Sooner or later she would cross the river and have the life everlasting.

"Yes, dear, what is it?" A child was pulling on her arm. With a rush of warmth, like circulation coming back to a numb limb, Harriet left the chilly upper reaches of the world-to-come, and leaned down to whisper to her grand-nephew.

"No, not yet, Syd. They're just playing music. It's kind of draggy, yes, but there will be ice cream and cake later. Wait a minute."

Not quite proper, but what was the harm, she thought, as she fumbled in the drawstring bag on her arm for a box of crystallized ginger. She might be old-fashioned, but anyway the children liked her. And until she was ready to partake of the inheritance of the saints, she could partake right here and now of her inheritance on earth.

Chrissie

". . . *in the face of this company, to join together . . .*"

Chrissie felt the same shiver down her spine she used to have at the theater—that moment of sudden hush when the wall of curtains cracks and ripples back.

"*. . . this Man and this Woman . . .*"

How strange and impersonal it sounded. Not like Sally, her old school friend, her roommate at college this first year. Sal in blue jeans; Sal in her absurd shortie night-gown; Sal with her hair done up in curlers. How could this be Sally he was talking about?

"*. . . these two persons present come now to be joined. . . .*"

It might be anyone—these two persons—Mother and Dad before she was born. They were young once, too, like her. They had been in love, too, like Sally and Mark; they must have stood up just like this, heard these same words.

"*I require and charge you both, as ye will answer at the dreadful day of judgment . . .*"

But somehow it hadn't worked. And Mother had said it all over again with Spencer, not so long ago. She remembered the wedding, in a blurred sort of way, though she wasn't quite grown up. It was queer watching your own mother get married, to a stranger like that stepping in—a stepfather, odd word. Was that where it came from?

Not a stranger, really, though—her stepfather. She liked Spencer. But it was a funny kind of wedding, two middle-aged people for the second time—not like *this*.

Could they have felt like Mark and Sally? Spencer was almost bald, and Mother was a darling; but really—she *was* thickening around the middle, and that wisp of hair, always falling down behind her bun. It couldn't be love. Love was something else, something much more exciting, that she felt tingling in the air, the room, the flowers even, today. Something that was happening to Sally—

"*. . . wilt thou have this Man to thy wedded husband . . .*"

And it would happen to her, too. Soon, soon, Chrissie hoped; she could hardly wait. Yet, in a way, she was glad it was all ahead of her, still untouched and unopened, like Christmas as a child; or a dance not yet begun, where you knew you'd have a marvelous time, but all still ahead, waiting for you.

When would it start? This year? Next year? Was it possible she might be married this time next year? To whom? Someone she knew—someone she didn't know? Someone in this room?

Her glance fell on André opposite her, the only possibility around. You sort of expected the best man and the bridesmaid to pair up. He was good-looking, too, in a way; dark, mysterious, but always that slightly supercilious smile. And when he talked— No, not possible—he took himself so seriously; she got fed up after a while. Not her type, at all. Even Mark was more her type.

But where was *her* Mark? She couldn't imagine him; yet here was Sally's Mark just a few feet in front of her, standing up there large as life, about to marry Sally. They'd hardly met a year ago, and here they were linked up for good.

"*I, Mark, take thee, Sally . . .*"

Sally—Mark: the personal names, said in Mark's personal down-to-earth voice, came as a shock in the midst of the impersonal service. These weren't two strangers, a picture bride and groom. God, they were her two friends, Mark and Sally, getting married. It was all real. Unbelievable, but real. Mark's voice was real enough, and strong, too. His jaw was set and he spoke up, loud. He was sure, all right.

He'd always been sure, Chrissie remembered, from the time he saw Sally on that ski weekend in Vermont. A born pro, Mark—on the surface, anyway. Just had that look about him. They'd noticed him on the slopes before they met him, the long dark line of him, erect but actually leaning forward in perfect balance. And those neat little flicks of the feet like a bullfighter or a dancer, as he christied to a stop.

Of course he'd noticed Sally too. Who didn't? That blonde mane flying in the wind. He'd been serious from the beginning, but Sal wasn't sure. There were so many boys. They used to sit up in their rooms in Freshman Hall and analyze them, she and Sally, night after night, while she did her fingernails and Sal put up her hair in curlers. How callous they were, picking over them like cherries in a basket, turning them round and pointing out their black spots, without a qualm. Invulnerable, they were then, on top of the world. She would never be able to do it again—gloomy thought—at least, not with Sally.

But in those days, they weren't in love; they didn't care. Boys were just there to be picked over, to be typed, for the fun of it. Who invented the types she didn't remember. It was part of their private language, those four labels: Sparklers, Twinklers, Worthies, and Lumps.

Everyone had a couple of Worthies hanging around. Worthies were sons of your father's and mother's friends. Old dependables, the big-brother type. You didn't mind their seeing you with a cold or your hair unwashed. Not exciting, but definitely ahead of Lumps. Lumps were usually other girls' cousins brought in at the last moment. They were just Lumps to everyone. Everyone knew them on sight; Lumps were unmistakable and never changed, while Worthies, of course, were relative. You never knew. One girl's Worthy might be another girl's Twinkler; you couldn't be sure. Twinklers were definitely attractive in a quiet way, and usually improved on the third or fourth date. They had a good sense of humor, too, which put them ahead of Worthies. Sal always said she liked Twinklers best.

But Twinklers never swept you off your feet, like Sparklers. Sparklers were it for Chrissie. You knew them right away, like Lumps, but at the other end of the scale. They were the big men on campus, the football heroes, the show-offs sometimes, too.

Mark wasn't a Sparkler. Sal had said from the beginning he was a Twinkler. But honestly, Chrissie wasn't too sure. She sometimes thought—feeling like a traitor—maybe Mark was just a Worthy in disguise. Not that she would dream of saying that to Sal—not any more—not now.

Did you *have* to marry a Worthy, Chrissie wondered? Or even a Twinkler? Not her. She wanted a Sparkler, even if Mother said they were unsteady and would never settle down. Mother *was* settled down, that was the trouble. How could she remember what it was like when you were eighteen? How it felt when someone rushed you who . . .

Oh—Chrissie's thoughts slowed up as if frozen midstream—*Dad*. Had *he* perhaps been a Sparkler? Was that why it cracked up—Mother and Dad?

She couldn't think back that far, couldn't trace her way into the years before the divorce. It all seemed covered with snow, that landscape. Now she was in another landscape, different, peaceful like farm country, but flat and uneventful. Things were pleasant at home with Mother and Spencer. Was Spencer a Twinkler? For Mother, maybe. Steady, yes, but dull. Not her type, that's all.

The unsteady people— Well, she had forgotten most of the loneliness when Dad went away. She only remembered how exciting it was when he turned up suddenly, as he used to—just appeared like that, picking her up and taking her out for a spree, to the theater; letting her gorge on chocolate éclairs and sodas; or surprising her with a new bicycle or a party dress that Mother could never afford.

And then, of course, he left her again. God, it was awful. She could remember how that hurt. You always hoped it would never end. "This time for keeps," you said to yourself—and then he left, without a word, for months on end. She used to lie awake wondering how he could love her and leave her like that, or whether Mother had sent him away. Mother always disapproved of the chocolate éclairs (they made her sick the next day), and the impractical party dress—and *certainly* the yellow roadster he had given her at graduation. Perhaps Mother was jealous, Chrissie thought, afterwards.

Just the same it was wonderful when Dad turned up at school and whisked her away for the weekend, or took out her friends to the most expensive place in town! "He's terrific, Chris!" The girls played up to him like mad. He could do the Charleston; he remembered what it was like to be young; he still *was* young. They were all dazzled. "You're so lucky, Chris!" She used to think so, too. But he went away. If only you could have someone like that, not just for weekends, but for good, for keeps—

"*Bless, O Lord, this Ring, that he who gives it and she who wears it . . .*"

Sally's hand was held out to Mark, a little white hand from the white silk sleeve. But it was trembling, Chrissie noticed. Poor Sally! Was she so frightened? She had been before the ceremony, and almost stumbled going down the living-room steps—just the way she had at school graduation. They'd been walking together then, Chrissie remembered, and Sal caught her heel on the gym steps and would have fallen flat if she hadn't grabbed her arm.

But she couldn't do that any more. Sally was gone, turned away from her, lifted into another world, of wedding dresses and husbands and honeymoons. Were you still frightened in that world?

Would she be like this herself, Chrissie wondered, standing before the minister? What made you so trembly before marriage? What were they all afraid of? It seemed such a terrific step, "unto their life's end." So irrevocable, "till death us do part." How could you be sure he was the right man?

There must be a right man somewhere, like the right coat waiting for you, hanging on a rack in a store. With a coat, all you had to do was to try it on and look at yourself in the mirror. Then you and your friend and the sales-girl all said, "It's *perfect*—just *perfect*, dearie."

But you could always send a coat back, if it wasn't a sale and your mother had a charge account. But not a husband. No "on approval" there. And how could you know? Was it instantaneous, like the movies? Your glances met "across a crowded room," and then "you knew"? But that had already happened a number of times to her, and once they got together in a parked car she hadn't known anything. Of course her stomach turned over when she got kissed; but that was just sex. Or was that all there was to it?

How could you tell if it were the "real thing"? Would the "real thing" be utterly different and new—on another plane altogether? Or would it be just more of what you knew already, and had been through ever since Junior High? Would it be a gradual, safe sort of thing—the boy next door you'd known all your life, and one day realized you couldn't live without? Or would it be the stranger coming silently toward you at a party? He would take your arm, almost roughly, and you would follow him and you would know, "This is it."

But would you really know? That was the trouble. If only there were some sure way to tell, like floating rotten eggs or rabbit tests for pregnancy. There weren't any real tests for love and marriage. Nothing you could count on. You couldn't even ask anyone.

You could, but what was the use? The girls she and Sal knew who got married right out of school—none of them would admit to being anything but blissfully happy, except for the desperately unhappy. And you couldn't talk to them; they were soured for life.

It looked as though people just wouldn't tell you the truth about love and marriage. No one ever had enough experience to get wise or have more than a prejudiced point of view. And the mistakes were so ghastly. You'd spent all your money for the coat and when you got it home it wasn't perfect after all; it wasn't your coat, and it wasn't even returnable. You were stuck with it.

Of course, it *was* returnable. There was divorce. Mother was divorced; but who wanted to wait till middle age to be happy? What was the use when your life was practically over? It must be so different then. Mother and Spencer in love—there was something ridiculous, almost indecent, about it. How could two middle-aged people "cleave" to one another? And repeat those phrases, and feelings, all over again?

Falling in love after marriage was out—no matter what the books said. Before marriage, of course, you were supposed to fall in love over and over again until you found the right person, until the "little bell" rang in you. Suppose the little bell just didn't ring? Or suppose it rang all the time, every time a boy made a pass at you? How could you tell what was the real thing?

It was different in Mother's day, as far as she and Sally could figure out. No nice girl ever sat in a car with a boy then, or got kissed until she was proposed to. But now, if a boy took you to the movies and didn't try to kiss you good night, you felt sort of insulted.

Their mothers never fooled around with boys at all until they got married. Maybe when they were engaged, but they didn't even admit that. No one told you what it was like, making love—how you just didn't care what happened. You never got the whole story. Even in modern novels, or psychological studies or statistical reports. They talked all around it and isolated it and delimited it; but the vital point was always left out. Just like those first sex movies they showed at school when she and Sal were in seventh grade.

What a farce it was, that evening. Mothers and daughters were supposed to go together. But a girl would rather die than sit with her mother. Only the drips did that. She and Sal sat in the front row, giggling and drawing faces until the lights went off. The mothers were in the back, knitting and gossiping. They all watched those clear little diagrams of the uterus, and the growing changes in the female form, clicking away brightly on the screen. So neat and tidy; not the vaguest resemblance to flesh and blood. Then the lights went on again and everyone blinked and sat very still.

"Are there any questions?" Miss Abbott asked crisply.

No questions—what dope would ask a question?—only the complacent click of knitting needles in the back of the room.

"Did you understand, dear?" Mother had asked later. "Sure," she remembered saying. "Sure." She understood all about what happened when the little sperm met the ovum. It was perfectly clear in the picture, everything running up and down those little grooves. The only thing was, they never told you how the sperm got *in* there, in the first place.

It was all like that, the real thing left out of sex, or love. Of course, she knew she was naïve as hell. No wonder, brought up alone by her mother. You couldn't ask *that* generation; and she was ashamed to let on to other girls how little she knew, though they'd been discussing it for years—love and sex, and all the stories that went around. She didn't have any stories, but she listened like mad: what could happen at drive-ins; how far you could go; who had and who hadn't; long arguments about safe periods and foolproof contraptions and ghastly accidents. The girl who got caught and went abroad, and what happened to *her*.

The funny thing was, they had their morality, though Mother didn't think so. Really, Chrissie thought, they were a lot more moral than the older generation, in spite of—perhaps because of—their experimenting. They had to have rules to protect themselves; nobody else protected them. The rules didn't stop experimenting, but playing around with everybody was out. Even as far back as Junior High, to go steady was the ideal. It made her mother shudder. But wasn't it good, really? She still felt that way, even now.

All the girls she knew wanted desperately to be faithful, to have just one person to be sure of, to be true to, forever. They felt much more strongly about it than their parents. Lena said it better than anyone. She got married right after graduation—too soon, everyone said, but Lena was sure; she knew. Chrissie would never forget that afternoon sitting in the tiny bathroom, with Lena bathing the baby. She didn't even have to ask questions; she just sat there, breathing deeply of the warm fragrance of baby oil and soap, listening to Lena as she had never listened to her mother.

"You just can't discuss it with your parents, Chris," Lena had said, her bare arm cupped under the baby's head. "They're so tied up. They can't help it; that's the way they were brought up. And then" (she removed the baby deftly to her toweled lap) "they're so terrified you'll get pregnant, they just panic; they only tell you the ghastly consequences. They never tell you anything *good* about sex."

"If they did"—Lena hesitated a moment, rubbing her baby's head against her cheek—"maybe we'd understand why it was better *not* to go too far."

"They never tell you—" Lena hesitated again and Chrissie wondered if she was going to be told anything after all.

"They never tell you how wonderful it is when the right man makes love to you." Lena flicked the bathinette cover back over the tub and started dressing a wildly kicking baby. "Each part of your body comes to life when he touches it, as if it had never been alive before—as if it had been asleep, or stone that suddenly is turned to flesh.

He brings it to life. It's a kind of miracle," she had finished.

Chrissie remembered how she tingled all over then, tingled still when she thought of it. Lena went right on folding and pinning diapers. "But if you let everybody do it," she added, "just fooling around—well, then the miracle doesn't happen. There isn't any miracle."

It was the miracle they believed in and were waiting for, Chrissie knew. She still wanted to be waked like Galatea in the Greek myth. The marble would turn to flesh at a kiss; but it had to be the right person, as Lena said. There was only one destined for her, approaching even now, she felt, riding inevitably toward her—just like an old-fashioned Western. It was terribly corny, but this was the way she always imagined it—someone riding toward her. She didn't know his name or what he looked like, but she was sure he was coming and she would recognize him. He wouldn't be like any of the others; not like André, so solemn over there, or Chuck, who was a hot-rod, or Bill, who had a string of girls and you could never count on, or Mike, who kissed her once and went away—well, a little like Mike. He would be for her alone. And she would recognize him, somehow, like a theme song in a ballet. She'd know when she heard it.

So far, she'd only heard it at a distance. Sometimes she felt it coming closer—when Mike had kissed her. Or times like this at a wedding, she felt it coming—always the same: like a spring night with the windows open and the soft breeze blowing the curtains in, lifting them on a great tide of sweetness and warmth. Spring and love and life were blowing in the windows, lifting the curtains, flattening her skirts, almost lifting her off the ground—

like the slow movement of Beethoven's Ninth, honeyed, haunting, rising.

It is coming, the music said.

Yes, but what was coming? Who, oh, who? And when?

You didn't know. You wouldn't know till it came. But it was coming inevitably, Chrissie was certain. She could rest on that. It would come as surely as spring, as surely as the future was rushing toward her. As surely as this service was rushing to an end and Mark was lifting Sally's veil to kiss her.

Chrissie felt the tremor that was going through Sally; it was going through her too. She shut her eyes, and felt it in the pit of her stomach as if the whole earth was turning over inside. Like sex—like a baby moving inside you, perhaps. Chrissie felt it sweep over her in anticipation.

Oh, she breathed, it will come to me too, to me too!

André

"I, Mark . . . thee, Sally . . ."

Mark was speaking. The familiar voice of his friend startled André to embarrassed awareness. He was in an American living room, André remembered now; it was afternoon, and Mark was getting married.

He pulled himself back from the drowsy anonymity into which he had slipped with the first resonant tones of the marriage service. This was Mark, his friend Mark, whom he had taken to France on Oncle Pierre's exchange plan, in whose family he had lived this year. His best friend over here. After all, he was the best man, wasn't he?—whatever that meant in America. He was certainly in his best clothes, and so was Mark, standing up there a few feet from him, repeating those words. Why did it all seem so unreal? A strange service, read by a strange minister, in a strange language.

Though it was *he* who was the stranger in this room, André knew, and not the other way around. It happened often enough, yet he never got used to it. Here he was again, in the center of an American family, at an intimate home ceremony—one that few Americans would be asked to in France—and he felt, as usual, a complete outsider, a stranger, alone. Of course, he wasn't alone. He had come with Oncle Pierre. If it hadn't been for Oncle Pierre—

André glanced at his uncle's stocky form next to him, the prominent forehead, the sparse hair receding from the temples, the keen gray eye—not a twinkle of humor in it today. Oncle Pierre wasn't enjoying this any more than he was. They were both strangers, though Oncle Pierre had been here most of his life teaching, except for the war years. How could he bear being away from France? It was hard enough, André thought, just for a year as a student.

Not that people here weren't cordial to him. Americans were always cordial. Everyone accepted him as Mark's friend. Here at the wedding all the members of Sally's big family took him in as a matter of course. The stranger was welcomed immediately in America, with enthusiasm even, into a large entrance hall, and then—well, then, it seemed to André, he just stood around, expectant and bored, never advancing a step further.

For a long time André felt he was being kept out of the small inner room where the real life of American families went on. Not that he minded, exactly. Naturally, he was excluded from the *intimité* of an American family, as an American would be in France. But somehow, that hearty welcome seemed to promise a little more—the tingling handshakes, the honest look on those bright young faces.

He had just been through it this afternoon. All these kind people pressed his hand warmly and looked deep into his eyes, like an initiation into some sort of brotherhood. Over and over again it happened. And then the usual good-natured neglect followed; you couldn't help interpreting it as exclusion.

But perhaps it wasn't exclusion; perhaps Americans really were as cordial as they seemed. They opened every door and gave freely of what they had. Was there simply nothing more to give? Nothing else? Just this noisy semi-public *salle d'attente*, where everything took place, and no quiet inner room at all; no *intimité* in the sense of a French family?

Even in Mark's own home—he knew it so well—he never found the inner room. They were good friends, of course, but it didn't give him any sense of a home. Mark's mother he adored, but not really as the center of a family, the pole of a house around which daily life revolved—more as an individual. They were all individuals, it seemed to him, loosely but reluctantly tied together into a family group.

Mark, too, had always been an individual to him, apart from his family, until today. Today—quite a shock, really—here he was, the center of a great patrimony. In his dark blue suit over there, solemn, erect, good-looking—suddenly transformed into the ideal young man, the son of the house, to whom everyone turned, on whom the family would lean.

Quite an entourage, Mark's family, André thought, looking from face to face. He had never seen them together before. How much Mark shared with them, at least physically. His friend's familiar traits were reflected on all sides, like a composite picture, diluted and distorted among these relatives. Here was Mark, softened into the feminine in his sister and mother; Mark, contracted into old age in his grandmother; Mark, blown up by success and middle age in his uncle; and finally—was it possible?—Mark, blurred by dissipation in his father.

Did all this lie ahead for his friend—his free gay friend? No, oh no, unbelievable.

But the real Mark, where was he? The young college boy who spent the summer with him in France. Mark, as he first met him—shy, then, the way young Americans are shy; not stiff and reserved like the English. When you broke through the shyness, he was blurtingly honest and naïvely eager to make friends, to talk.

How they had talked, over two beers at a sidewalk café, with great excitement about books and ideas, philosophy and politics; then rather stiffly and cautiously about their lives and families. Last of all, André remembered, those spasmodic break-throughs, fascinating and astonishing to both of them, about girls and dating. That was when he first heard about Sally, a glamorous, faraway figure, like some budding Hollywood starlet, flitting across the screen.

There were others, too. How lucky they were in America, André thought. Making love was so easy, even in their teens—all those parked cars, and boys and girls going off for weekends alone. So different from the way he'd been brought up. No girl he knew at home would dream of such a thing—not at that age, anyway.

Here in America they grew up fast and married early. Look at Mark, barely out of college, no profession yet, no career started—standing up there getting himself married. Fantastic! A French boy would think it mad. Couldn't afford it, for one thing. Of course Mark had money; that made the difference. How many years, André thought, before he could support a wife! Not so many over here. America was the place to make money, everyone told him. Oncle Pierre was urging him to stay.

He'd like to, in a way; he'd get ahead faster, get married sooner.

But even so, did he really want to be in Mark's shoes, already settled down, and for life, too, with one woman? No more flitting around for Mark, deciding in each capital of the world which girls had the best legs or the prettiest faces. A respectable married man, his role was cut out for him from now on. Poor Mark. André began to feel sorry for this sober young man standing in front of the minister.

He tried to imagine his friend's future: Mark as the responsible father of a family, sitting at the head of a table, reprimanding his children for misbehavior; or Mark as a sedate citizen, walking to church on Sunday morning, or digging in his garden and pruning his fruit trees Sunday afternoon.

Did Americans do this? No, probably not; they cut their lawns in shirt sleeves. Well then, pushing a lawn mower or a baby carriage. No more dashing about for Mark; no more doubts and confusion. He was rooted in his own plot of ground.

The roots and the plot of ground, André rather envied. But not Sally—not Sally at all. He glanced at her now, standing beside Mark. Fragile and delicate, today, charming in that flowery lace; but it was a kind of masquerade. She was really a gay tomboy, competent and attractive, more herself in blue jeans, with her page-boy haircut in the wind.

No, American girls were not for him. They were attractive enough, pretty, friendly, like Chrissie who rushed at him last night. (How they did rush at you, American girls!) And he was certainly lonely; but they could not fill the void. Sometimes he found himself walking the campus of a girls' college, unconsciously repeating the words copied as a child in his English notebook: "Water, water everywhere, but not a drop to drink." His mood exactly. American girls could not fill his thirst.

Why not? What was it? They weren't really girls, he kept feeling. Outrageously frank and uninhibited like children, but no real consciousness of being women, or even of sex—in spite of their strapless evening dresses and Freudian language and freedom in parked cars. They were playing with sex, he always felt, like little girls dressed up in their mothers' clothes. Or—no, more like little boys, playing at war, tossing ammunition about, not knowing what it was, or how to handle it.

French girls were different; more of the coquette in them perhaps, but less aggressive. They knew the rules of the game from the beginning and played it more subtly. They expected to be treated differently from boys, to be complimented and given a few attentions, even a little gallantry. Otherwise, what was the use—or the fun —of being a woman?

They knew instinctively, French girls—Paulette had known even when she was twelve or thirteen—what it was to be a woman. She took it for granted he would treat her like one, and enjoyed it. Over here if you took out an American girl and gave her a compliment, she was apt to throw it back in your face and laugh at you, like Chrissie last night.

Chrissie and Paulette—what worlds apart they were. Paulette at this distance made him think of some early spring flower he used to find in the woods at Easter, that belonged only there in his forest and would die transplanted to this metallic hemisphere.

But an American girl—he just couldn't imagine marrying anyone who didn't have the background of France, like a tapestry, behind her. A French tapestry, with its soft colors, its embroidered *millefleurs*. The colors of an American girl wouldn't fit there. Too garish and bright. How could you put a girl in blue jeans against a French tapestry? Blue jeans were everywhere, even in Paris, but it offended him to see them.

Oncle Pierre was lucky; he had found a French girl willing to go to America with him. He and Tante Adèle had gone together and carried their tapestry with them. It was part of their home, the only place in America where he felt at home. Not that it was very European, that garage apartment. Rather modern and bare, actually, their big all-purpose living room under the eaves, except for Adèle's copper pans in the kitchen corner and Pierre's paper-backed books stacked untidily on shelves up to the ceiling.

Yet the room had a warmth to it, a living warmth, as though a fire were burning in the grate to welcome him. But then, he had never come into it empty; there was always someone waiting for him, either Tante Adèle or Oncle Pierre. He was expected, wanted; he could sit down as if he were going to stay; he could stop running, relax, breathe more easily.

With a base like this, perhaps one could live in America. It was certainly the place to work, to get things done. Mark was right about that. In France, one was still tied down by those cobwebs of habit. A great gale of energy swept one along in America. Was this still the pioneer spirit Oncle Pierre talked about, always pushing outward?

But how could one live here? André came back to the same conflict. Could he ever reconcile himself to this world of speed and emptiness? The American home didn't seem to possess the inner core that attracted members and close friends in France, or in his aunt and uncle's home here. Where would he find it, then? Back in France? Here in America? And with whom? Had Mark found it with Sally, pledging to hold it for life? For life! Could one ever keep it? His aunt and uncle had, but who else? He glanced around the room full of strangers. Mark's mother, the beautiful Frances?

He looked at her now, standing across from him. Not exactly the picture of a happy woman, he realized suddenly. Surprisingly frail-looking, too, today, for all her strength. It must be a strain on her, losing Mark, it occurred to him for the first time. She was, in spite of all her admirers, curiously alone. And rather old, he noticed, catching a glimpse of her face, in repose for once, not animated as it usually was in conversation. He noted analytically the gray hair, the sagging lines under the chin, the slight suggestion of pouches under the eyes, and a certain indiscriminate washed-out color to the skin itself.

Not really beautiful at all, he summed up, and probably never had been. At best, no more than *une belle laide*. And yet, so charming, such an illusion of grace and beauty— some of the innate wisdom of European women, combined with the freedom and spontaneity of Americans. Wasn't it this he wanted in a woman? He didn't envy Mark his wife but he did envy him his mother. Not as a mother, though, he realized. As a woman. What a shame there were no young girls in America like Frances. American women did not seem to develop this kind of ease and grace until they were too old to make love to. Such a pity.

He had been staring at the frozen image of Frances, with complete impunity, as one might stare at a statue. Suddenly the statue moved. Frances lifted her hand to her cheek as if to brush off a fly—or a glance.

André started from his trance. Suppose she turned and caught him staring at her! Would she read what had been in his mind? He had actually imagined her in his arms. He felt the color rising in his neck. Would Oncle Pierre notice? Stiffening to a glazed formality, he projected his glance over Frances's head to the bridal couple in the window.

In the cool cave of this safe corner, he rested, caught his breath, and came to himself. His heart was beating as though he'd been chased at hare and hounds, or waked from a nightmare. Perhaps he'd been only half awake. An absurd dream, imagining Frances as a young girl. She was as old as his mother. Besides, he wouldn't be seeing her any more now that Mark and Sally were married.

"With this Ring I thee wed . . ."

André watched Sally bow her head and Mark take her hand. The two stiff figures in the window, carrying through their pantomime in slow motion, looked dim and far away, abstracted like dancers in a ballet. He was only an onlooker now, observing their drama, no longer a participant in their scene or a member of their family.

But he had never really been there, had he? Relief and regret met midway in him. He would say good-by to them all, he decided with a rush of feeling, turn his back on this alien world.

Raising his chin still higher, André looked beyond the couple now, beyond the minister, and above the rambler roses in the window, at a little corner of the summer sky outside. Too clear, too glassy bright for a French sky, he observed, but still, free open sky.

The escape was so complete that André felt his immediate surroundings drop away. The sights blurred out; the sounds hushed to stillness. He was somewhere else, on another planet. It was a few seconds before he realized that it was not just his corner of sky transporting him; the room itself had undergone a change. The sounds of the service had ceased; now gently, imperceptibly, filling the silence, were the first tentative notes of music.

What was it? Oh, what was it?

André kept his eye on the little scrap of sky in the window as though it could enlighten him. He felt transfixed by the first few notes rising, familiar as the voice of his mother, seductive as a wave of oncoming sleep, or tears; but faceless—faceless because unnamed.

And though he reached in anguish for the name, as one fumbles for one's bearings waking in a strange room at night, he knew that as soon as the music yielded its secret identity, its power would collapse and ebb away. Only this unknown, unnamed stream had the magic to summon him from wherever he was and transport him, naked and defenseless, to another world.

He was a child in bed in his old room upstairs alone. The slatted persiennes were folded like wings over the long windows, bolted against the dark outdoors, but not closed to the pungent smell of rosemary growing in a high bush outside his window, not closed to his mother playing the piano downstairs below him. He had a half-nibbled piece of chocolate, out of an American war *paquet*, hidden under his pillow. He felt fed, by the chocolate, by the music, by the sense of his mother, recaptured, somehow, not separated from him as he feared a few minutes ago, when she left him. She was not, then, really beyond the closed door and bolted persiennes. She was still with him, pervading the room, with the music, with the smell of rosemary.

But the music—what was it? Bach, surely, but *which* Bach? The opening melody started again now, climbing like a sunny goat path up the terraced olive-planted hills of Provence where he used to visit his grandmother. He was pursuing it, as he used to pursue those paths as a boy, crushing the pungent rosemary and thyme underfoot as he climbed. Those paths kept tempting him up one terrace more, to get a little further from his home—the tile roof under the yellowing plane tree, the smoke from the chimney rising, a straight blue thread in the early morning stillness. A little more height, now, and it would be left far below.

Once past the olive trees at the steep part of the hill, he had to make his own path, clambering over rocks, pushing through the bristling bushes, scratching his bare legs as he fought his way up, until finally he reached the rock, the flat rock, in a little nest of gorse, behind the big single pine. Here, secret, sunny, and still, he would sit for hours, safe from any prying eyes, enclosed by the thick mass of bushes with their redolent yellow flowers. He was in his own fortress, yet the valley lay spread out before him. He was separated from the cramping details of daily life, yet he could survey them all.

But the tune called him back, firmer now, in the base. It was something he knew well, not simply at home as a boy; he had played it lately. When, he wondered, and where? Perhaps at Oncle Pierre's, lying on the living-room couch at night, listening to records in the dark, only the firelight glinting occasionally on Adèle's copper pans or lighting up the overflowing shelves of Pierre's books. Half asleep, the music beat in his temples, while shadows advanced and receded in waves on the ceiling, and arguments fenced in his mind. How could he reconcile the old world and the new, bridge France and America?

There came a moment when the tide of shadows and the climbing notes merged into one pattern. The two opposing voices in his mind were reconciled. He could distinguish both voices and perceive how each answered the other. Both were equally valid and could coexist in him. He could encompass them both.

Then again it was like the hill at home; he was not torn in pieces, but whole. The worlds were not separate, but one. The music, the smell of rosemary, the sense of someone loved were not shut out by the closed door. His valley and its scents, his village and its sounds were not lost by the distance he had climbed. The near and the far were spanned in one glance.

Expanded by peace, by beauty, by music, his mind seemed able to take in all kinds of opposites: absence and presence, the near and the far, America and France. He could not lose the things he loved most, no matter how conflicting. They met in him, fused in him—at moments like this. It was possible, then, for moments anyway. This moment. Now.

Ah—the final chords paced off the end of the music—he remembered at last. He had played it himself, the second one in the book. He could visualize just how the notes looked on the page. How simple—how stupid not to remember.

That was all. It was over. The room around him stirred faintly to life with a rustle of coughs and scuffings. Chrissie was looking around, trying to catch his eye. He stiffened guardedly. No, she was looking for someone else, her mother, perhaps. One was suddenly aware of all these other people in the room.

He was not in France—André straightened himself—not in the apartment. He was here, in a room full of strangers, alone. No, not alone. There was Oncle Pierre beside him. They were both alone. They could console each other.

André turned to face his uncle.

But what the devil was he so happy about—Oncle Pierre? What was there in this occasion to make him so happy? What could there be in life to make anyone so happy!

Beatrice

"Who giveth this Woman to be married to this Man?"

In the slight stir that followed, Beatrice shifted her position to catch a better glimpse of her daughter. She could see Chrissie's taffeta dress shimmering just behind the bride. They were in the back, she and Spencer; not relatives, just friends of the family. They had come really more to see Chrissie as bridesmaid than to see the bride. Spencer, too, bless him, even though he wasn't Chrissie's own father. He stood by at times like this—*Who giveth this Woman . . .*

John McNeil was stepping forward to the bride. Stiff, unbending, hiding his pride and his tenderness behind that stern mask—a gray crag of a face—but he was *there*, there next to his daughter. Sally had her father's strength behind her.

Chrissie! Beatrice realized, with the shock of truth, Chrissie could never have this—not her own father. Because of the divorce, because of her, it would never be the same. Of course, divorced parents did appear at weddings. She and Tom could arrange it, but it would be artificial, just a form, really—never like this. She had deprived Chrissie of having her father's strength behind her at her wedding.

A body blow—why had she not anticipated it? Beatrice drew herself up and took a deep breath to counteract the sudden weakness, as though her strength were leaking away in a hidden wound. Was she going to faint or collapse? Absurd. She never fainted. And Spencer was right there next to her—her husband, Spencer. Her real husband. If she felt dizzy, if she swayed, he would put his arm around her. He would hold her steady.

She had only to look at him to be sustained: the smooth temples where the sparse gray hair had thinned away, the veins showing through the fine skin now; the feathery wrinkles around the eyes from his humorous squinting glance; the mouth, bent a little crooked in the pull between determination and compassion. He would respond with a glance.

Even without a glance, she could put out her hand. They had touched hands instinctively as the service started. All she needed was to touch him, to tap that strength, the common strength they gave each other. And yet, at this moment, she couldn't move a finger, or reach out, or ask for a drop of his strength. Not here.

This was her problem, not his. You didn't ask your second husband whether you should have stuck by your first. Suppose Spencer admitted to her that he occasionally wished Kitty back from the dead? No, you didn't pull the rug out from under your partner. You didn't share everything. Certain problems had to be carried alone. She had carried her load; she would continue to carry it. There were no real doubts. She had been right, after all. Right to divorce Tom; right to marry Spencer. But in an unguarded moment like this, she could still feel remorse; strength running away into might-have-beens, quicksand under the feet of a wrong decision. Not for herself—no, her own small plot of ground was firm under her feet, and Spencer was standing right there with her—but for Chrissie.

Chrissie had been deprived, the moment told her. To what degree? How could she gauge the hollow in her child? To look at her, standing on tiptoe behind the bride, as though she had just lit there like a will-o'-the-wisp, everything was all right. Everything was gay and tip-tilted; crisp curly hair, eyes turned up at the corners, slanted, pucklike. Irish eyes, quite a bit like Tom's, really. To look at her, you wouldn't guess a thing was wrong. How could it be? She was bouncy as the Light Princess, floating up to the ceiling. It was often hard to pull her down, hard to get at her. Always laughing, Chrissie; like a wound-up music box, the tune tinkling everywhere she went. And yet, Beatrice couldn't help wondering, what was hidden under that laughter? People could laugh on top of awful things. She remembered those gay tuberculars she'd seen somewhere in a sanatorium, laughing with half a lung. Did Chrissie have only half a lung? Half a heart? Was she crippled in a way they couldn't see?

She still felt guilty at times like these. It set her back years. Divorce seemed so dreadful, especially at weddings, and when you started looking back. "Divorce is amputation." The phrase rang in her from the past. Who had said it to her, in those years when she was struggling with her decision? Only the phrase remained. Slowly a face blew up around it like a nightmare. An older woman—she couldn't even remember her name—just the mouth, bitter and hard, with lines at the corners, as though sewn in like a buttonhole to keep from smiling. "Divorce is amputation," she had said with that button-hole mouth. "Don't give up until gangrene sets in."

Gangrene! Hideous image. Not for her. Mock-heroics weren't her style. Beatrice had decided then and there she wasn't going to wait that long. Just to show you were in the right and had done all you could. Imagine—sitting there holding on in sheer pride, waiting for blood-poisoning to show up. What a way to save a marriage! If it had to be saved like that, was it a marriage?

But was it a marriage, anyway, with Tom disappearing for months at a time? On press assignments, of course. Perfectly legitimate. She knew all that when she married him. A reporter, especially a top-flight one like Tom, had to be taking off for Hong Kong or Korea or Burma, wherever the pot was boiling. It wasn't his going as much as the way he went. The suddenness, the compulsiveness, as if he *had* to go, as though he couldn't bear to stay around a second longer. The assignments began to seem like excuses. She suspected him sometimes of inventing the crises abroad, or ferreting them out, so that he had to leave.

And when he left, she was shattered—for years she couldn't figure it out. It wasn't just the trips. Spencer went off now too, for meetings and scientific conferences; but he never seemed anxious to go, or else he wanted her along. It was different. Spencer always left her something to hang on to, almost tangible: a lifeline, that never quivered at all, no matter where he went. He didn't destroy the connections between them each time he left.

With Tom, the whole structure of their marriage shattered to smithereens each time he slammed the door—as though he wanted to destroy it. That was the real trouble; he wanted it destroyed. At least for a while. Then he'd turn up again unexpectedly, for shelter, for food, for warmth; to hole up between assignments, under this roof he didn't want to build, didn't bother to support. How could marriage exist under conditions like that?

Wasn't marriage something two people built together and held together, patching it up here and there when it needed repairs? A definite structure, part of the pattern of society. A social institution, if you came down to it. Rather an unromantic view, perhaps, but this was the way it chalked up to her. Constructive or destructive? she asked herself, when she looked around at other marriages.

Not happy or unhappy. She didn't ask that question. The best marriages, like the best lives, were both happy and unhappy. There was even a kind of necessary tension, a certain tautness between the partners that gave the marriage strength, like the tautness of a full sail. You went forward on it. It was constructive—one had a right to ask a marriage to be constructive. Most of them were, surprisingly enough; something endured.

Look at Deborah and John standing there side by side—a married pair if she ever saw one. How indissolubly knit they looked today—and were, too, though Debby never seemed quite grown-up. She was still that snub-nosed, round-eyed girl she'd known in school. Not much changed. Usually a little breathless and panting, as if she'd lost twenty minutes somewhere during the day and had never quite caught up. Beatrice would always remember Debby, arms full of books, scuttling down halls. "Did you get our Latin assignment? I was late to class and didn't dare ask." Debby was still like that. She never got into any real trouble. There was always some-one to ask. People invariably helped Debby. She was dis-organized but sympathetic, like everyone's younger sister. Maybe she was John's younger sister, too.

And John—dear John—loyal, staunch, conventional. Beatrice would never forget how good he'd been to her in the years between her marriages, helping her with the divorce. Perfect as a lawyer, John. You knew you could put it all in his hands and trust him completely. He never asked unnecessary questions or probed into painful places. He had his standards and he understood what was necessary. Kind and firm, he pushed things through. Of course, you could never cry on his shoulder, and there were lots of things you couldn't say to him. He had blinders on, in a way; needed them maybe, dealing constantly with people's problems, not to get too involved. Perfect for a lawyer, but for a husband—per-haps a little distant? Did Debby mind? But, after all, that's what she wanted when she married him, someone to give her the Latin assignment.

Not the most mature couple, as the books would say, but they had a real marriage, whether they knew it or not. Consciously or unconsciously, they had made a web of relationship that held and fed their children. To-gether, too. Accidentally, blindly, even grudgingly some-times; but they had done it together.

That marriage worked, despite Debby's complaints. She was always in a dither about one child or another, always worrying and asking advice. Jake was left-handed and Susie was a cry-baby. John spoiled the girls and was too hard on the boys. Beatrice had listened to her for hours.

"But he cares," Beatrice used to protest when Debby complained of John's temper. "Don't you see? His children matter to him. You should be glad he gets angry; he cares. Tom doesn't care."

Debby and John both cared. Was caring enough? Those children had turned out quite well, despite Debby's worries and John's temper. They knew where they stood with their parents. John was a rock, and even Debby, under that flurry and worry and wrinkling of brows, had a surprising amount of strength. Only she didn't know it, or didn't believe it and needed it confirmed. She had never taken a good look at herself, and perhaps John wasn't perceptive enough to give her back the true picture. This was what she wanted. Debby's complaints weren't really asking for advice or sympathy, but for confirmation, not simply of each act, but of her truest self.

Confirmation is what we want, Beatrice realized; what Spencer gave her without complaints, without her asking; what she gave him without ever thinking about it; what Tom had never given.

Perhaps he too had taken her complaints at face value and wanted to escape? How could she blame him? You couldn't expect a man to be Almighty God and see into your hidden motives. No wonder he ran away, to work, to play—to other women, sometimes, she knew. Those rumors she only caught the tail of as she entered a roomful of people; those women she never quite saw. But that wasn't what destroyed a marriage. At least, she could have forgiven Tom that—maybe even understood. "I know I am but summer to your heart," she used to repeat to herself at night, "and not the full four seasons of the year." She was much too tame for Tom. A field of summer grass would never hold him, never in the world.

But adultery wasn't the worst sin against marriage, as somebody said. Who was it? Milton—could it have been Milton? Adultery didn't destroy marriage as much as "unmeetness." *Unmeetness* described it exactly. She and Tom couldn't meet in this mutual web. In fact, it was the web itself that scared him. He shook it; he tore loose from it; he turned his back on it. He denied it existed.

Did men tend to look on marriage as a trap, while women saw it as a frame? Both concepts were false, because both saw marriage in terms of one person instead of two. She couldn't make a marriage alone, just as Frances would never make one with Stephen, running away into alcohol. It was the same thing, though Frances couldn't see it. She saw only the good periods of her marriage, when Stephen was sober and working. Each time he started painting again, she was sure it would last forever, but it never did.

Too bad Stephen was ever sober, really; it kept Frances from getting a divorce. She hung on to that little thread of normality and made it her whole life. No matter how often she was disillusioned, she never learned; she never saw the true picture.

Why not face it realistically, Beatrice had asked her the last time Stephen collapsed. Either divorce Stephen and make a new whole marriage with someone else, or just settle for half a one—marriage with an invalid, a child. That's what he was, Stephen. Better accept it; and then go get yourself a good steady love affair outside. Right to Frances's face, she'd said it.

What a thing to tell a friend—or to remember at a

wedding! Beatrice looked around uncomfortably at all the conforming couples. How coupled everyone looked at a wedding, dark shoulders of men against women's light flowered dresses; black against white, fixed as a keyboard. What a heathen she was. It was the years struggling alone, outside of the safe circle. The code had become blurred and tangled; not black and white as it used to be, as it still was to most people. To the church, the world, and society, her advice was blasphemy. How could a love affair be "good" or "steady," or acceptable on any grounds?

A sin, then? Certainly not right; not what she would want for Chrissie, not the whole and perfect web marriage was meant to be. To destroy the web was a sin. She believed that, too. But everyone didn't have a whole web, sometimes only remnants. It seemed less of a sin to add another thread—that's what an affair was—another thread to tie up the remnants. Terribly imperfect; two halves didn't make a whole; nothing like perfection. But didn't perfection sometimes stand in the way of reality?

For Frances, it did. No half measures for her. It was all or nothing. She would go on beating her head against that wall forever, thinking she'd find a way through, like a bumblebee against a windowpane.

Such a mistake, Beatrice thought, a hideous waste, waste of energy and life. You felt it more strongly as you grew older, if you'd found happiness a little late. The lost years looking for the wrong things, believing the wrong things, these she regretted—the years before she found Spencer. Frances was making the same mistake, losing her strength, getting old with the struggle.

Beatrice shifted imperceptibly closer to Spencer to

catch a glimpse, over shoulders, of Frances in the front row. Rather drawn, she looked today, in that dark dress, Beatrice thought; too pale, with circles under her eyes. She was erect, though, her head held high, almost too high, pulling taut lines under the chin. It gave her a look of gallantry.

Beatrice felt suddenly humbled before her friend. Maybe Frances would find a way through in the end. How could anyone tell—she, least of all. Who was she, anyway, to judge a marriage, or a man? How could she doom one or the other? Or look into the future? She'd never been able to see ahead in her own life. And looking back, over all those stumblings down and hoistings up, if she'd learned anything, it was that you died and were reborn many times.

A process the young couldn't imagine. They saw the same tubby gray-haired parents, getting tubbier and grayer through the years. The new growth didn't show on the outside. Who could believe it? The person Tom abandoned had died. The person Spencer loved was reborn. And Spencer, too, after Kitty's long illness—those years of devotion—had gone underground with her death.

And yet he had come back, could read her that poem the other night about the shrivelled heart. In front of the fire with the Oxford book between them, Spencer had read her: "Who would have thought my shrivelled heart could have recovered greenness?" Two middle-aged people by the fire, with a dog-eared book between them— who would guess that what they were reading was explosive, the explosive power of life's renewal?

"And now in age I bud again," he read. No one saw the buds, but they were there. "I once more smell the dew and rain." Unbelievable, like morning. "And relish versing, O my only light—" O my only light—how incredulous you were when it came, when life started again.

> "It cannot be
> That I am he
> On whom thy tempests fell all night."

But were they the same people? How could they be? The person who married Tom—who was she? Beatrice really didn't know; didn't know now; knew even less then. She tried to think back to her school days. They were brought up then—she and Deborah—to want a career, to be outstanding in the world of women, to make their mark. How could she tell, back there, who she was? Florence Nightingale, Louisa May Alcott, or Anna Pavlova? She must have been very young at that point. And there was the person whose candle burned at both ends. And a girl with a green hat. One of these, was she trying to be? Which one did Tom see and fall in love with? And whom did she see in Tom?

It took years of stripping away the illusions, the poses, the pretenses, before she knew who she was, the naked humble human essence. And then to be able to reveal this essence to another human being, to be accepted as this—to be loved, even, as this, by another person who dared to show himself in all his naked vulnerability.

Here I am (this was how Spencer came to her), a gray-haired, middle-aged man, who wanted to achieve greatness and who has only achieved the capacity for patient work, a little success, and some wisdom about life; who has suffered and failed often, and sometimes won; who can offer you what he is—and who loves you.

Heartbreaking, the way Spencer came to her—but a real person. Only two real people can meet. She and Tom hadn't met; she and Spencer had. But would she have noticed Spencer back there in her school days? Or even looked at him—one of those shy tall boys with glasses. Would he have recognized her under those Clara Bow ear-puffs? Beatrice wasn't at all sure.

This was why, she realized belatedly, you could never regret the past, call it a waste, or wipe it out. All loves led to the final love, to the final stripping away of the unreal selves, to the true meeting.

It was certainly best if it happened before marriage. With Pierre and Adèle it was like that, love at first sight. They had recognized each other immediately at a student meeting; no doubts at all, married in a month.

Were these people just lucky—the love-at-first-sight couples? Or were they the clear and the whole, who had found themselves early and could meet others without masks? She wondered about Mark and Sally, and how it would be with Chrissie, when she found her unknown. At least *that* generation had fewer illusions to strip off. No ear-puffs, anyway.

But sometimes the meeting took place outside of marriage. For Frances, it still might happen. Or even in the middle of a marriage; Debby and John might someday find out who they really were and recognize what they had together. Or in a second marriage like hers, the meeting started a whole new growth, another life.

Not a whole life for her and Spencer; almost half a life unshared. She minded not sharing their youth, not knowing Spencer as a young man, taking chances and making mistakes. Would he have been more adventurous if he'd married her first? She wished they could have kicked off their shoes and run through the grass together—perhaps lain down together in the grass. The excitement of first love, the fierce mingling of their bodies, young, they had missed.

"With my body I thee worship," she remembered from an old version of the wedding service. Her own interpretation, she supposed, but here was the heart of marriage. She understood it better now she had a marriage rooted in the earth of a good physical relationship. Something she hadn't known with Tom, hadn't even missed because she didn't realize it existed. It wasn't just physical attraction; she'd had that intermittently with Tom. It was something steadier, more continuous and taken for granted—physical expression. It wasn't complete, of course; they hadn't had a child.

If only they could have had a small Spencer, looking like the boy she never knew, bean-poly and leggy and intense, collecting turtles and snakes. Though it might have been hard on Chrissie, a half brother, Spencer's own child. It was hard enough as it was. Chrissie had lost a father and nothing could quite make up for it—not even Spencer. Wasn't that clear enough today? There was no use pretending.

At least, Chrissie had seen a good marriage; she knew it was possible. She had seen her mother relax and become another person, her real self, perhaps at last a real woman. For years, Beatrice knew, she had tried to be both father and mother, both a man and a woman. Impossible, of course. You couldn't give what you didn't have, or be what you weren't. It was somehow false, a kind of fancy-dress. You kept tripping up in those borrowed clothes. Or else you learned to wear them too well. They forced you to act an unreal part, forced you to be a man.

Was this why Tom left her? The question stirred in her uncomfortably. But, Beatrice found herself protesting inwardly, she had tried so hard to be a woman when Tom came home; not to dominate, but to be open and warm and yielding, to wait and to listen. She took off all her armor, when he came home; but when he left, as he always did, she had to put it on again, those breastplates and knobby knee-greaves. She needed them to stiffen into a man, to fight, to press her way against the world alone.

It was different with Spencer. She had taken the armor off for good, now. She could stop struggling so desperately, let him buffet the world part of the time, instead of bulling it through alone. After you had struggled alone for a while, you had more respect for men's problems, those inexorable burdens of earning a living, holding a job, and the responsibility for a family. She'd had enough of it to know; she could sympathize with men's reactions to women's gripes. They always looked so trivial, women's worries, but weren't they every bit as immediate and physical and daily? The trouble was, so often the surface worry, like Deborah's complaints, hid some enormous problem underneath. Only the tip of the iceberg was visible. And there were always icebergs. What were Tom's flights, and Stephen's drinking, and John's temper if not tips of icebergs? And what was her own fierce housekeeping in her first marriage?

That iceberg, at least, had disappeared. It didn't seem to matter any more, having the house spanking neat and efficient as a factory. Other things mattered. She wasn't quite sure what, but she found herself spending mornings on the most ridiculous things: arranging flowers, for instance, scratching her arms and legs to gather black-berry blossoms. The whitish leaves were just the right color under the Cézanne print.

She had even taken to studying cookbooks, digging up new recipes. Always before, she had hated cooking. Children take eating for granted, and you don't cook for yourself. But cooking for Spencer, pleasing him with a favorite dish or surprising him with a new one, was one of the rites of the day she most enjoyed.

Housework, she had discovered at this late date, had to be a gift or an art, otherwise it was sheer drudgery. For her now, for most women, she realized—at least the happy ones—it was a gift offered in love, not an art perfected in pride. Perhaps this was why, it occurred to her, women usually are good cooks but rarely, according to the French, great chefs. Love moved them rather than pride.

How late she had come to this common-or-garden knowledge of women! How topsy-turvy it was, in middle age, to feel like a young bride—or the way she imagined a young bride might feel—about these dull and un-important details. Ridiculous at her age, reduced to being "domestic as a plate."

But were these things unimportant? Small, yes, but weren't they significant? These daily details weren't just gifts to the other person; they were contributions to the common roof you shared, like the spears of grass and bits of mud and gay scraps of string that robins bring to build their nests. Wasn't it this, when Spencer put up a bird-feeding station she could watch from her kitchen window, or when they bedded down the roses in the fall, or grieved over a winter-killed root?

The endless small interplay of daily tasks couldn't be called trivial. Wasn't it the substance of life itself, the web of marriage, as important as the bigger things, even an expression of them? These ordinary gestures expressed a whole rightness of feeling and being and meeting—expressed *meetness*, as Milton said; this was what he meant.

Yes, she had met Spencer late, but they had truly met. It was such a miracle that it hardly mattered whether it was in first or second marriage, whether in youth or middle age. Whenever it happened, it was the true meeting, the true marriage. Those who truly meet, meet here, meet now, meet in God, she felt suddenly with unorthodox certainty. They are the people God has joined together, and the only ones, whom no man can put asunder.

For the first time this phrase at which she had always flinched—where the divorced all flinch—was comprehensible. It didn't shut her out; it included her, too. She was rejoined to the human community, not that any of them realized it. No one would understand her smiling at this phrase; they might even think her bitter or callous. Except for Spencer. He would understand; he would know. She didn't look at him; it wasn't necessary. She dropped her hand very lightly to touch his at her side.

Pierre

"Our Father, who art in heaven . . ."

The wedding guests, separate individuals up to this point, thoughts wandering, glances straying, became, with the first lines of the Lord's Prayer, a single body. All random actions were channeled into a unity of bowed heads; all coughs and scuffings drowned in a muted chord of response.

The low anonymous chant, listened to with closed eyes, presented a frieze of sound; the familiar background for any congregation, any church, anywhere.

Even a church in France, Pierre thought, instinctively following the phrases in his own language. *"Que ton nom soit sanctifié."* Would André also be repeating the words in French? He glanced at his nephew beside him. André's head was discreetly bowed. It was his first American wedding; Pierre wondered what the boy was thinking. *"Donne-nous aujourd'hui notre pain quotidien."*

Our daily bread, echoed Pierre, seeing again the long, hard French loaves of bread, sticking out of his mother's black shopping bag when he was a child. He could still smell the moist aroma of freshly baked bread, a warm blast of air that met him when he opened the door of the *boulangerie*. How enviously he had eyed the little soft rolls, on the glass shelf, that were only for Sundays.

Adèle bought them for him, now, if she passed a French bakery. If she had time, she would make him brioches for Sunday breakfast. What a joy, those leisurely Sunday breakfasts, when he didn't have to rush off to class.

Now, of course, with Adèle away, Sundays were just like other days, only worse. No reason to lie in bed; no reason to get up, even. He preferred weekdays, when he was off early to the university. With his students in the lecture hall, or at his desk in the library, he didn't miss her as much. He was used to being alone there.

But coming home at night—frightful—especially climbing up the stairs to their garage apartment, cold, unlighted, empty. No delicious smell of soup, and Adèle's voice floating down to him, "Ah, Pierre, at last—"

He knew she had worried about leaving him for this month. "Are you sure you can manage without me, Pierre? I don't believe you ever cook when you're alone. Don't get into the American drugstore habit; you need a good hot meal at night."

At her suggestion he had taken to eating at the university these past weeks, coming home late, directly to his desk and unfinished manuscript. His book—at least he could work on that while she was in France. Almost too much work, as Adèle had foreseen. "You will stay up the whole night at your desk if I'm not there to pull you to bed." But what else was there to do? She deserved this time with her family; and, while he wouldn't choose a monastic existence, with work to do it was tolerable, even profitable.

But to go to a wedding without Adèle, a festive occasion like this—Pierre was still protesting inwardly. Of all places to be without one's wife—a wedding!

Yet, almost her last words as she got on the boat were: "Be sure to go to Mark's wedding, *chéri*, and remember everything to tell me."

Why wasn't it enough for André to go? he had asked. Surely their nephew could represent them? Their nephew, almost a son, the son they never had. Pierre had repeated this last only to himself, though Adèle was probably thinking the same thing.

When there was an abyss in one's life, an open pit in the garden, one could never forget or overlook it. One walked around it carefully each time; quietly, though, not complaining, not crying *watch out* to the other person; just skirting it casually and silently, as if it weren't there.

Adèle hadn't mentioned it either when she answered.

"But it will mean so much to Frances if you go, Pierre," she had said. "She has been so good to André. You can go together, you two."

He sensed something else unspoken in her plea, stronger than her words. *It will be good for you*, chéri, *to go out a little—not to be buried in your books so much. You can flirt with Frances and have fun and feel less lonely.* Had she said it out loud he could have protested, but as it was—

All right, all right. Of course he would go with André. But still, it was not the same thing, not like going with Adèle. How could she have thought so? She was treating him like a little boy, sending him off in his best clothes, with a pat on the shoulder, as his mother had done years ago.

That time his mother was ill—he must have been quite young—he remembered having to go alone with his father to some celebration. Maman had said, "It will mean so much to Tante Félicie; you two men can support each other." Just like today, he felt embarrassed and resentful, as though something were being put over on him. But he had gone, done his best to be polite, made the proper excuses for his absent mother, upheld the family honor.

"And how did he behave?" his mother asked on their return. "*Admirablement!*" his father laughed. "He lied like an ambassador!"

What a joke it was in the family. Forever after, too. He was sent on every social occasion and referred to as *M. l'Ambassadeur.* It pursued him through his school days. They half expected him to go into the Foreign Service and earn himself the title, but he never did.

He never became an ambassador. The nearest thing to it was coming to America to teach. Wonderful country, America, so open, vigorous, whole. Vision wasn't split from action, here, as it often was in Europe. A healthier state, *du point de vue morale.* And if the American vision didn't always see far enough—well, that was where he came in. This was the job of teachers. Perhaps they were ambassadors, bridges between the two countries. He'd been a bridge all his life and believed in it. André would be a bridge too, he hoped, if he could stick it out. He was rather lonely, just now, poor boy, but that was natural enough.

He'd been lonely, too, Pierre remembered, when he first came to America. Before Adèle. Those bleak years in a boardinghouse, before he was married, before he'd even met Adèle. How lucky he'd been to find her—in his own home town in France, too—willing to come with him, unafraid, open.

She stood out from the others at that student meeting,

less complacent, readier for adventure, fresher. There was a kind of simplicity about her—not the bucolic kind, but what Fénelon was talking about: "an uprightness of soul that prevents self-consciousness." *Upright* was precisely the word. Even physically it suited her. Like a candle flame. No, less wavering. Like a young tree. No, less rigid. Like a fountain, springing up straight into sunshine. She even made him feel more erect when he came home tired or discouraged. It was enough just to look at her, to have her by his side.

But she was *not* by his side in this living room, not here at all.

Pierre felt the weight on his shoulders again, the burden of being single. It made one stoop apologetically, and stay in the background; an uncomfortable sensation of being naked and unprotected, yet actually cramped in one's best clothes.

Ridiculous. Why hadn't he stayed home where he was still surrounded by Adèle's things—her pots and pans above the stove, her geraniums at the window; even her penciled slips of paper pinned to the wall, reminding him, in her swift birdlike writing, how much milk to order a day and when the laundry came and where to pick up groceries. Her touch was still there; her absence a sustained, unbroken note, curiously comforting, as though time had stopped until they met again. Here, in this crowd, he couldn't hear the note, except intermittently. He couldn't even miss her properly; she wasn't a part of it.

Ah well, he was here and must make the best of it. He could watch the ceremony, notice the guests, remember to tell her about it when they met in France—only two weeks left, now. No, he would write her tonight.

Adèle, *ma chérie*, I went quite dutifully this afternoon to Mark's wedding, just as you said.

What would she want to know, now?

The bride, yes— Sally was charming in—

But then, they always looked the same—brides. Fragile and feminine in white lace.

And Mark? Mark looked serious. Didn't all grooms look serious?

The wedding party? Frances was very chic—

Naturally, my dear, Adèle would say. She is always chic. Now what did she wear?

He couldn't see very well from where he stood, just her head.

Well then, the others?

Let me see, the McNeils, Deborah and John—

The parents of the bride, he could hear Adèle being sarcastic. *Naturellement!* I rather expected *them* to be there. Was he taking it hard—John?

John? Why no, I didn't notice that. (Adèle always noticed everything.) He seemed much the same, dignified and silent, as always. Deborah, now, I would say *she* was nervous—

Of course, outwardly. (He could hear Adèle holding forth on this subject.) She is always nervous, but the wedding is harder on him; here she is stronger. (Adèle had odd ideas about things.)

Tiens, you know, do you? You have the eye of God, Adèle?

No, but I have an idea. (That would settle that; then she would go on to something else.) Who else was there— the Maestro?

Formidable, as usual. *Magnifique*, with his great shock of white hair, always acting a part, conscious of his audience. Why must artists be such egotists, Adèle?

But they aren't all egotists. (She would disagree.) Some of them aren't egotists enough—look at Stephen.

Yes, you are right, Adèle, Stephen doesn't believe in himself. He has no mask to hide behind, either, except drink. He was sober at the wedding, though. Quite presentable, you will be glad to hear. Fortunately for Frances, though she was surrounded by friends.

What friends? (Adèle was always curious.)

That doctor and his wife, some kind of psychiatrist, you remember? A strange fellow; they are all a little strange in that profession, in my opinion. His wife too, do you agree?

Don and Henrietta, you mean? (They almost always agreed, but Adèle might challenge him here.) She is unhappy, that is all. Life has cheated her.

But *how* has it cheated her, Adèle? (This would be an argument.)

It is obvious. Her sister made a better match. Her husband doesn't love her; he is unfaithful—

But, Adèle, how do you know? (He had to take a stand, sometimes.)

Ah well, I know.

Are you sure? Have you proof?

Of course not; one doesn't need proof. I know—

But really, Adèle, you shouldn't say things like this if—

To others, of course not, but to you— (She always had the last word.) Besides, it is obvious when people are happy. Look at us. Look at Beatrice and Spencer—

Ah yes, the Lockes, I forgot; they were there.

Beatrice and Spencer, they both came? (This would please her.)

Naturellement. Everyone was there with his wife, except for me. I was alone. What a position to be in! A wedding is not an occasion to go to alone, as I said, Adèle. One wants to share it; to stand with one's wife, looking at the bride and groom, with memories in one's heart.

Can you remember, Adèle, what it was like, twenty years ago—our wedding? You were beautiful; but so formal suddenly, framed in that stiff white stuff. I was startled, quite frightened, really—not of you, but of the form. It is the form that frightens us, the picture we have of marriage. How can I ever be married, as Papa and Maman are married? Impossible! Or Oncle Jean and Tante Félicie? *Jamais.* I am not ready for this. Oh no—

But, after all, it was *you*, Adèle. And there you were, upright as usual, unafraid. With *you*, it was possible. I never should have got through it without you.

Évidemment! (She would laugh at him, but she would be pleased.)

You laugh, Adèle, but this is the point. One doesn't have to be married in the same way as anyone else. In fact, it can never be the same. Each couple creates it afresh, like these two today. And yet, there is something universal—*n'est-ce pas*, Adèle?—the eternal striving to become one; the dream, realized only in flashes, of total communion.

Two solitudes, who protect and touch and greet each other?

No, this is Rilke, Adèle. You know how I feel about your beloved Rilke. Too Germanic, too mystical for me. Besides, so inaccurate. *Two solitudes:* a beautiful phrase;

but not communion. Two people facing each other, talking to each other—this is communication. Saint-Exupéry was closer to it, you remember? "Love does not consist in gazing at each other, but in looking outward together in the same direction." Still not communion, though; only communication of a kind—what poets care about most.

But, Pierre, even for us, who aren't poets, surely communication is part of it?

Of course it is, *chérie*, it is. Who was it who described marriage as a long, continuous, many-stranded conversation, shared over the years?

And how you worried about this conversation—do you remember, Adèle? Whether we would have it or not? You wondered what we would talk about in the evenings. As though it could run out, what we had to say to each other; as though the only communication were in words, when really—"*Être avec les gens qu'on aime, cela suffit*" (this is it, *chérie*, it is enough to be together): "*rêver, leur parler, ne leur parler point*" (it isn't necessary to speak), "*penser à eux, penser à des choses plus indifférentes, mais auprès d'eux, tout est égal.*" This is it.

If Adèle were here, he wouldn't have to say it. Simply turn and look at her and know she was thinking the same thing. They would join in the throng afterwards, shake hands, congratulate the bride and groom, drink a glass of champagne—probably not French champagne, but still, champagne. Then they could go home—home, where he could take her in his arms. Their early married life came back to him: rushing home to her; throwing themselves in each other's arms. The true homecoming, like touching one's own country, after long exile—

But this was too stupid; he was alone. Why was he torturing himself?

Pierre turned to look at the other couples in the room, the lucky couples, side by side: Deborah and John, Don and Henrietta, Frances and Stephen. He felt a curious chill, a sudden drop in temperature of his wedding excitement. What was the matter with these people? So cold and joyless, these couples; so separate and rigid, standing stiffly side by side. All but Beatrice and Spencer. What had happened to the others? Was each one a special case, like Frances? Or was there something wrong with marriage in America, as his compatriots were always saying— still under the Puritan blight; the men too inhibited as lovers, the women hungry and frustrated; discontented and dominating, like Frances.

Unfair, probably; but just the same, Pierre hoped André wouldn't marry an American girl. Though Adèle would disagree. Don't be foolish, she would say, all American women are not like Frances. Frances is unhappy.

But she was more than unhappy, Pierre thought, glancing at Frances as she stood a few feet ahead of him. She looked hungry and driven. The rat of discontent was gnawing away at her. Always had, he suspected, and probably always would. A difficult woman to love, even to flirt with. How silly of Adèle to imagine it. She would never be satisfied—not with a man certainly—driven by something, a dream, an impossible ideal.

Frances made him think of an untalented Simone Weill, forever analyzing, dissecting, rejecting; and forever seeking. Or those women Rilke wrote about whose only complaint was that they were asked to limit their giving. In another age, perhaps, Frances might have found an unlimited vocation to claim her. But, as it was, she seemed condemned to an endless search, a pursuit of perfection that overlooked the human possibilities, the solutions of ordinary people; the church, or a love affair, or even divorce. Too much Protestant pride, perhaps. She could not accept help from others; she had to do it alone.

But we are not meant to do it alone. We are meant to do it together, *n'est-ce pas*, Adèle? Pierre turned back in relief to the inner conversation with his wife. What is marriage but this: to accept one's humanness, one's inter-dependence? To accept help from another as well as giving it—just as one accepts God's mercy, whether one deserves it or not.

Not that I deserve it, Adèle; I don't feel I deserve your love, but I accept it. I even take it for granted like my daily bread. Too much so, perhaps. At times like this one realizes what it might be to live without it. Quite ordinary, our daily bread. One breaks it; one shares it; one eats it almost without tasting; but one cannot be without it, or live on crumbs, like Frances. One needs the whole loaf. And it must be good bread.

Do you remember, Adèle, my telling you, when I first came to America to teach, how I tried to save money by living on bread as I had at home, with coffee in the morning, with cheese at noon, with soup at night? And I starved; it wasn't good enough—factory-wrapped, not nourishing freshly baked bread.

But then, you weren't here, Adèle; we weren't married. I starved for this, for the bread of life, the living bread St. John speaks of in the Bible, that can be divided end-lessly and still nourish, like the miracle of the loaves and the fishes. The bread of love. Only love can be divided endlessly and still not diminish.

The love of God, you call it, Adèle, not the love of man?

But surely it is the same substance, though humbler. We partake of God's love when we love each other. The sacrament of marriage—it is this, *n'est-ce pas?* It was this we found, Adèle. Is it so hard to find? For us, it was simple. There it was for the taking—for the giving.

There it was in front of him, now, in that young couple, Mark and Sally. He could not help looking backwards to his own wedding, and projecting forward for these two in the window. What would grow from this moment of communion?

They will be happy, Adèle. They are like us. Why, she even looks a little like you—as you looked that day. It is the blondeness, the transparency of the skin. Yes, *chérie*, she does.

The pleasure he felt at discovering the likeness was so intense that Pierre turned involuntarily, looking for his wife beside him, to face—not Adèle, but his nephew, André, looking with astonishment at his uncle's radiant face.

Frances

"*Mark, wilt thou have this Woman to thy wedded wife . . . love her, comfort her . . . keep thee only unto her, so long as ye both shall live?*"

"I will," said Mark.

With the sound of her son's voice, the room stopped shimmering for Frances and came into focus at last.

This was better. She could stand still and find her way from here—like waking up as a child at night and steadying herself by that crack of light in her room. The hall light, it used to be, she remembered, gleaming weakly through the crack under her door. Such a long walk down the hall in the old house, to the bathroom at the end. Full of dangers, that passage at night, an ordeal, a sort of Odyssey to get to the dim ceiling light at the far end. You had to force yourself out of bed, hanging on to the thread of light, and march forward to safety and deliverance, like storming the kingdom of heaven.

I will. How strong Mark was! Even as a child, sitting on her lap, reading *Mother Goose*. " 'I will,' said the little red hen." Absurd nursery song. Mark had loved that one: the little red hen who did all the work alone, while the pig and the dog just played around. She was rather like the little red hen, herself, Frances thought. No one helped *her*—certainly not Stephen.

Frances could hear her husband's heavy breathing at her elbow now. Poor man, the wedding was hard on him!

Well, what did she expect when she married him—an artist, a neurotic who drank too much—how could he help her?

Mark had helped, though; done Stephen's jobs; carried too much, really ("'Oh, who will build the fire for me?' asked the little red hen"), bringing in the wood when he was much too small in the cottage on Long Island. ("'I won't,' said the pig; 'I won't,' said the dog.") Mark, digging out the front walk in winter, in his baggy snow-suit, with the shovel twice his size. ("'I will,' said the little red hen.") Mark, when she was off at work, taking Phyllis to school in the morning. Much more efficient than the mother's helper.

He was the mother's helper, of course. Too much so. She had leaned on him. She ought to have known better, seen more clearly. She made a husband out of him, per-haps even a father. She needed one badly then, before she learned you couldn't lean on anyone, not a husband, not even a father.

It was hard to grow up, to lose your parents; the breast, the shoulder, the strong arm. You kept looking for another one—another breast, another shoulder. Even in your own children, as soon as they could stagger under the load.

It wasn't fair. Children were too vulnerable. They *seemed* grown-up; they wanted to be. They stepped right into the role. Irresistible, to be mother's helper. Then they got caught. A trap, it was, a trap. *American women keep their sons in bondage*, she read somewhere. Wasn't it true?

The silver cord—yes—*silver threads among the gold, Darling I am growing old.* Those red-seal records they used to play on Sundays when she was a child. Filial duty, responsibility, guilt. And there they were, those good mother's helpers, caught in a box; dependent and resentful, crippled and rebellious, unable to marry—

"*I, Mark, take thee, Sally . . .*"

No—no! Frances shook off the nightmare. It wasn't true. Here was Mark getting married; not caught, not crippled at all, standing up there saying, *I will; I, Mark.*

His voice sounded so sure—how could he be that sure? How could anyone be sure at his own wedding? We all have blinders on until we take the step. Then we can see; then it is too late. Another unhappy marriage, and the pattern begins again.

How could she break the pattern for Mark, for Phyllis? Her own life didn't matter any more; but the children, the children's lives. This was what kept her awake last night, and many nights. Her children must be free of the pattern: unhappy marriage, endlessly repeating itself from one generation to the next. *Unto the third and fourth generation*, the sins of the fathers—

A sin? What sin had she handed on? Blindness, could it be? Perhaps it *was* a sin, when you analyzed it—not facing the truth, not wanting to look at the truth.

But the truth was hard to find, let alone face. Her whole life was a kind of journey toward it, trying to find it. Even now, looking back, did she see things as they really were?

A final look, these last weeks. Ever since Mark had told her about Sally, she had been looking back, trying to understand, for months now. But last night—dear God, what a long night!—lying rigidly awake next to Stephen, all the mistakes of her life flooded over her. In mobs, disorderly mobs. No beginning or end, the way it always is at night. Thought in the thickets of night, confused alarms—ignorant armies—clash by night—by night—

By day, it was different. By the light of day, the light of little sleep, everything cleared up. Martialed in order today, her thoughts; clear images, one after another. No fuzzy edges, no astigmatic blur of guilt or blame. The intensity of the moment burned all that away. A procession in the desert, her life raced past her today, sharp-shadowed in the sun.

Her unhappy marriage—she could see it now. For years she couldn't. Something was wrong, that was all she would admit. Not the marriage, not she, not Stephen—just *something*. Then, of course, she had to find out what the something was.

Stephen, she blamed first. Naturally. Married to a man who went off on binges—what could she do? God knows, she tried; tried to pull him together, to get him to a doctor; finally went herself. *Helpful hints on handling alcoholics*, that's want she went for.

It was really not to find out what to do, but *why?* Once you asked *why* and kept looking, it went deeper, always deeper. First the mote in your brother's eye; then the beam in your own eye. A neurotic husband; then the neurotic in you who picked one to marry. *Why* had she married Stephen? She wasn't sure even now.

Anyway, she no longer blamed Stephen—or herself. That came next. It was easy to blame yourself; it made you feel you were accomplishing something, a kind of substitute for understanding. But there wasn't any substitute. You had to try to understand, not blame anyone: Stephen or his parents or her parents, or even herself. Blame was just shifting the burden from one shoulder to another, shoving it further and further away, pretending you were doing something.

Fake action, that's what blame was, beating around the prickly bush you didn't want to enter. But there was no use avoiding it. You had to jump right in, like the old man in *Mother Goose*, who scratched out both his eyes. You had to jump right back and scratch them in again.

Sight, keeping your eyes open, was always painful. But once you opened them, you couldn't shut them again. The pictures came anyhow, as they did last night, flashing memories, like a night train journey through forgotten landscapes, jolting awake constantly to familiar stations, lit with unfamiliar lights. Last night the pictures were on her closed eyelids; today, eyes open, they were still there, even clearer.

Father, now—she could see him as he always was, through a dim cloud of cigarette smoke, good-looking, tired, charming, in his den, a fortress of books and papers, carefully guarded by Mother. She and Pete were warned to tiptoe around this inner sanctum, not to run upstairs, not to shout out the window, always to play baseball in other children's yards. "Your father is working at his book." "Your father has one of his bad headaches."

This book of Father's—what was it? No one ever saw it—never published. On the eighteenth-century diarists, maybe. He'd been a lawyer once, she remembered dimly, but that faded out. He went less and less to the office, and finally not at all; he just sat in the den, his retreat, his cap and gown. It gave the house an air of culture in that small upstate town.

But what did they live on? Looking back now, Frances wondered. Always on the edge, she knew. Grandpa had money; Father was an only son. That must have helped. And Mother made every penny count.

How Mother worked—such energy, her missionary background—up and down the stairs with her head wound in a duster, baking pies for the church fair or wrapping old clothes for the lepers in Allahabad. Mother ran everything in sight: the house, the children, the town. "When Mother lifts her little finger, you know, we all tremble"—Father's old joke. Something to it, though.

Was Mother happy, Frances wondered? You never knew exactly. Everything was so hidden under all that activity. What did Mother feel, really feel?

Father, now—you knew what Father was feeling—sometimes so charming, telling slightly improper stories of the eighteenth century, flicking cigarette ashes over the carpet—for Mother to pick up, poor Mother. Sometimes sitting at table, hardly saying a word, just sort of mumbling to himself. A broody hen, Mother called him then. Nobody called it neurotic in those days. "Despondent" was the word, or just "run-down."

Run-down, like a mechanical toy or an old clock; and Mother wound him up again. "Why not take a walk, Edwin, a quick bracing walk?" she'd say; or "What you need is a good spring tonic." That austere hexagonal bottle of Peptomangin on the bathroom shelf, or the fat sticky bottle of malt and cod-liver oil—those magic bottles.

It wasn't always enough. Father must have been very run-down the year they went abroad. Peptomangin wouldn't do, or a trip to the seaside. The whole family packed up and went to Europe—for Father's research, Mother said. That was smart of her. Better to brood away from friends and relatives. You didn't have to explain so much.

How you made excuses for your husband! "Stephen is working on a new project." "Stephen needs some new material." "Stephen is feeling antisocial."

But that was Stephen, *today*, Frances caught herself; Stephen, fidgety, a little paunchy under the eyes, standing next to her. *Who giveth this woman?* Thank heaven, it wasn't Stephen's job to give away the bride. All he could do to stand there; all she could do to hold him up, with her will power. As Mother had done at her own wedding, holding up Father, keeping him in hand, keeping him tidy?

But she wasn't really like Mother, was she? Frances stopped short at the image—like meeting yourself unexpectedly in a store mirror, thinking it was someone else, almost running into it. She wasn't really like that. And Stephen—?

No— Oh no, Stephen had been different—not like Father, not tired out. Completely different in the beginning. It was hard to go back—he had changed so gradually—to remember him as he was back there in Paris. He was the real thing, Stephen, when she first met him—a talented artist, studying at the Beaux Arts, too. Very good-looking, she remembered. He had a careless American boyishness, with a European sophistication she found fatally attractive.

She sat at his feet—how gauche and unsophisticated she had been!—and lapped up his world; a world she knew so little, but Father and Stephen prized. She wanted it, too. She was hungry, with the banked-up hunger of a small-town background. Europe was like a first spring day; light and color and warmth, after a long drab winter.

Dazzling, that spring in Paris. Stephen knew everything, saw everything. She saw with him, through his eyes. It wasn't like seeing things with Father and Mother, through a page of history, or the starred items in a guidebook, always secondhand.

Firsthand, this was. A whole new set of senses opened up to her. With Stephen, she ate and drank France: the silky spring green of the beech forests in Rambouillet, and *fraises des bois à la crème fraiche*; red wine from a carafe, and the rose window at Chartres. The beauty, the richness, the sad, exquisite weariness of Europe—how it seduced her! And the beauty, the sadness of Stephen, too.

Was the weariness also there, and she hadn't seen it? The European quality always drew her, even now. Any European—even Mark's friend, André. She turned involuntarily and caught a sideways flicker of André's pale intense face a few feet away. Poor boy, he was a little in love with her, too; but only as a kind of mother. What else could he see in her, middle-aged and gray-haired?

But even young, what had Stephen ever seen in her, back there in Paris? Uncultured, unsophisticated—why was Stephen attracted to her?

His first audience, perhaps. His older brother had all the attention in his family—Albert, the artist, the musician. But she had listened to Stephen, to his ideas, his dreams of accomplishment. It was easier to sketch them to her than work them out on paper. She took them all in, open-armed, like children; fed them, warmed them. And Stephen, too, in the end—Stephen, too.

He had proposed to her, Frances remembered, in that corner of the Bois where he had gone as a child with Albert. They walked down the same allées where he and Albert had rolled their hoops, trailed by a Swiss nurse. "*Attend, Albert, attend nous!*" Albert was always miles ahead, according to Stephen. He could never catch up.

The chestnut trees were still flowering that afternoon, the white dust of blossoms blown and crushed under their feet. Everyone was on the grass, like a Seurat painting, Stephen said; families picnicking under trees, lovers entwined in each other's arms, children twirling jump-ropes.

Jardin d'Acclimatation, that was the name. Why had he taken her there, past the miniature train and the toy boats, the flower beds and the Punch-and-Judy shows? Why to the children's part of the Bois?

Not to see the plants and animals, or the children. There was only one child in his mind that afternoon, the child he had been, the little boy with the hoop. They were really living in the past that day, until suddenly— they were walking hand in hand—he put the little boy with the hoop in her charge.

He stopped her, right there in the middle of the allée, and asked her to marry him. In the middle of the allée, they stood, their arms around each other. Nobody noticed; nobody cared.

And then they walked on, hand in hand. Nobody noticed. She hardly noticed herself; she had taken charge.

But she didn't know it, didn't even see the little boy with the hoop; she only saw her teacher and guide to this wonderful new world of Paris and spring. She wanted it to go on and on, endless new worlds opening up. How could she go wrong with Stephen leading her?

Then she discovered—it must have been when they got home to the house on Long Island—they were still holding hands, but *she* was leading *him*! How did that happen, the roles reversed? She was the parent and he was the child. At least, that was what Stephen expected—to lean on *her*, instead of her leaning on *him*. She wanted to lean, too. She wanted a father; he wanted a mother—and they woke up to find they were both children.

Just children, like these two at the altar today.

". . . *my wedded Husband, to have and to hold* . . ."

Sally was putting her hand in Mark's now. Hand in hand, like Stephen and herself.

Babes in the woods, she and Stephen had been, stumbling along, absolutely blind. When she began to open her eyes—it took a long time, years of moving unhappily from one suburb of New York to another—when she began to see, it was too late. There were the children, Mark and Phyllis; and Stephen, practically an alcoholic (". . . *for better for worse* . . ."). How could she get out of it, then? Would it have been possible (". . . *in sickness and in health* . . .")? She thought about divorce—a long time ago it seemed now—for the children's sake. But Stephen was a child, too! How could she abandon him? Mother would disapprove (". . . *till death us do part . . ."*). Father was dead by then. What would Father have thought? Oh, Father—

"Our Father, who art in heaven . . ."

What could she do? She got a job, out of desperation. That was a form of abandonment, too. But she had to get away. It didn't pay much, in the decorator's firm, but it gave her confidence and self-respect again. Pym did that, really, noticing her, going out of his way to make things easier. She and Pym—*that* was abandonment, God knows.

". . . forgive us our trespasses . . ."

Our trespasses— But it was inevitable, falling in love. Pym was her boss and watched out for her from the beginning. To be taken care of like that, when you were vulnerable, it was irresistible.

The day Pym took her out to lunch, they talked and talked; the restaurant emptied of people and there they were, alone over their cold half-finished coffee cups, still talking. The veil dropped between them. He was just as unhappy as she. Hildegarde was a possessive wife, hoplessly neurotic, always ill with some complaint or other. Was everyone unhappy? Was marriage a trap, too? How wonderful to find another person's hand to hold in this maze!

The comfort of another hand; that was enough, at first. She didn't ask where it led. She lived off nothing, like an air plant, a dream orchid. When it led to an affair (*". . . lead us not into temptation . . ."*), she woke up dazed and shocked. Incredible! How could her love for

Pym be called "an affair," just an ordinary shoddy affair like anyone else's? "Adultery," Mother would have called it—a sin, evil.

"*. . . deliver us from evil.*"

But Mother was dead then; and after the first shock it didn't seem evil, or even very strange. Stephen was her child; Pym was her lover. She and Pym both seemed happier, even better, for this secret life. No one seemed to suffer, in the beginning. She came home fed by Pym; everything was easier: children, work, husband. Even Stephen and Hildegarde got more love in a way. There was more love in the world—how could that be wrong? It overflowed onto everyone around.

"*. . . the kingdom, and the power, and the glory, for ever and ever . . .*"

But not for ever and ever— Oh no! It never lasts. Why do they say for ever and ever at a wedding? Only for a little while. Then something happens, something breaks.

What happened with Pym? Talking about marriage and divorce—*that* broke it. She began it, too. Pym always said how wonderful it would be, never to have to say good-by. But he didn't mean it, really. He never actually brought up marriage. He would have let it go on and on just like that, holding hands like children, going nowhere. It wasn't enough for her, holding hands forever in a maze, a dark labyrinth. She wanted to find the way out, unwind the skein of silk and follow it down the passages, like a light at the end of a long corridor, a crack gleaming under the door. Hand in hand, yes, but leading somewhere, out into daylight.

Otherwise, one lived in terror of being caught, the hidden terror, the monster who lived in the dark, who would catch you and devour you. Worse than divorce.

Divorce was terrible, but at least it was open. This hidden life in the dark—secrecy ate it up, belittled it. She didn't want it belittled. It must all be up to the level of their love, otherwise it was sin.

Yes, this was sin: not treating the big things in life—love, death, birth—with the bigness they deserved, with dignity, reverence, grace. Like a wedding, after all. It was so clear today. A wedding gave bigness, the bigness of God, and grace—"Giver of all spiritual grace."

But if you treated love lightly, shoddily, then it became shoddy and degraded, like her affair with Pym. Didn't Pym look at it that way? He belittled it, called it "a thing apart." The old saw about men and women. It had come down to that. Love was a woman's whole existence; with men—with Pym certainly—it was a thing apart. That expression on his face, she would never forget it; cynical, superior, slightly evasive, the day he threw the proverb in her face. "Oh, my dear," he had said, gently mocking, "you're not trying to make it your whole existence, are you?"

She didn't answer, didn't even try to answer, she was so angry.

Yes, you *did*—you did want to make it your whole existence. Why not? What was the use of breaking your vows for something light, inconsequential, merely pleasant? She believed in vows; it was terrible to have broken vows.

"*. . . and thereto I plight thee my troth.*"

Mark was giving Sally the ring, putting it on her finger. She believed in marriage, Frances felt with a rush of passion. She had failed once, but she still believed in it, more than ever. She knew what it meant after her failure. With Pym, she had wanted it right. She wanted love to be whole, not hidden and crippled. She wanted to start again, from the beginning, and go through to the end—till death us do part. Yes. Indissolubly one—

"*In the Name of the Father, and of the Son, and of the Holy Ghost.*"

Glory, how she must have frightened Pym! It wasn't *his* idea, at all, to be indissolubly one, linked with a golden ring, chained by a golden chain to a home. A home? Half-way house, that's where he stood. Not even a real house, a kind of summer pavilion suited him, a vined gazebo in the garden. He just wanted to stand there, protesting always how sweet it would have been, but not lifting a finger to make it real.

Not a little finger (". . . When Mother lifts her little finger . . ."). And when she threatened to make it real, how he panicked away! It was obvious, today; she could almost laugh. But that fall, she cried and cried. Hildegarde got some kind of arthritis and Pym had to take her to California. Total abandonment, she felt. Total disillusionment. Was Pym so different from Stephen? He didn't drink, but wasn't he just as weak, dominated by Hildegarde instead of by her? (". . . We all tremble . . .") There was the repetitive pattern again, terrifying.

No, she didn't want divorce. Not now; not for Pym; not for her. For some people it was possible. For Beatrice there across the aisle, divorced and remarried to Spencer. It was right for them. Other people, too, friends of hers— she had encouraged them—divorced, remarried, started life again; hurt but not maimed. Even the children—it was hard on them, of course, but they righted themselves; slowly, like bulbs planted upside down, but straightening as they grew. It was possible, divorce.

But not for her. Because of her vows, was it? At this late date? Was morality catching up with her at last, or was it just middle age and weariness descending?

No, not weariness, something more positive. Not even morality. Something else was pushing her, other values she felt dimly, on another level, deeper than morality. But what could be deeper than morality, more important than loyalty or keeping a promise?

Yet there was something deeper, she was sure; the value of life itself, perhaps—the growth and continuity of life. She only knew she must follow the direction of her growth, and yet, in following it, she mustn't shatter the wholeness of life around her; that small universe she had created despite herself, husband, children, home.

The moving forward toward truth, and the rooted-here of life's wholeness: this was the uneasy balance she had to keep. The two forces were always in conflict: the journey forward, the standing fast; the passion for truth, and the instinct to love. Was it like this with every woman? With Deborah? With Beatrice? With her own mother, even?

Or was there something alien in her, Frances, tearing her apart, pulling in opposite directions? Too much of the man in her, perhaps, wanting to go forward, running counter to the woman in her, who wanted to embrace and guard life.

But after all, she was a woman; the instinct to love was strongest. For a woman, love had to be grounded, in life and children and home. A man's love was different. Pym was right, then? How ironical! No, only half right. Perhaps the old saying wasn't bitter but trying to state a truth. Love was the same; but its direction, different. With a man it was the springboard for flight into work and outer creativity. A woman's love came earthward and had to be rooted. Here I stand, a woman said, and put down my roots and spread out my branches and hold up my fruit to the sun.

She was the tree, holding them all, Frances felt. How could she shake them loose, let them fall? Divorce would hurt too much; tear limb from limb: Stephen and Phyllis; she and Mark. Not only their flesh torn, but her own; not only their lives, but her own. The fullness of life—how could she have it, if she ripped her past from her, and her future? She was part of the cycle; she wanted to experience all of it; not just a segment, a little truncated segment of romantic love, over and over again. She wanted love, marriage, children and grandchildren; all of life a woman could have. The whole cycle—how could she get it outside of marriage?

Not in a love affair, certainly. A few years ago she was so sure. An affair was the open door to life. How precious it had seemed at first. Too precious, that was the trouble, like having just the heart of a flower; stamen and pistils, the most intimate part of a relationship—nothing else. Not petals or stem or leaves or fruit, or roots in the ground. How could it grow as marriage grew? Only marriage seemed to take in enough life, enough ground to grow on. And marriages, too, could wither, if they kept out life; they, too, stopped growing.

Was growth the criterion, she asked herself, for any relationship? And whatever stopped growth was a sin?

Everything looked differently through this lens, even her own marriage. After all, Frances had to admit, she had grown in her marriage; she was a little further along the road to understanding.

In her relief at reaching this outpost, she turned to Stephen at her side for confirmation. But his face was closed. He had withdrawn inside himself. Only the shell was left, the opaque mask she could never penetrate. She was alone.

This was the real bruise, the center of pain. She hadn't shared her growth with anyone. She and Stephen, except in the beginning, hadn't fostered growth in each other. They had grown, in spite of each other, pulled in opposite directions. No spiritual cross-fertilization; that germinating grain was lacking in their marriage. Could you recognize it ahead of time, teach your children to look for it before marriage, to pick out this grain from all the others?

But at this point—Frances looked at Mark and Sally, heads bowed in dedication before the minister—at this point, could you tell them the truth about marriage? Could you admit that yours was a failure? Their lives, all their growth was rooted in your marriage. You couldn't uproot them now, take the ground from under their feet. It would destroy their past, perhaps even their future, the lovely open sky of their future. Frances looked beyond the bowed heads to the window above, a little corner of clear blue sky. No, she couldn't cloud it with her fears.

Eternal love—they believed in it, Sally and Mark. They were pledging it now.

". . . *ever remain in perfect love and peace . . .*"

Mark was so sure; Sally was so trustful. *Ever remain*—how could you say to them: If it works for ten years, it's enough? *In perfect love and peace*—tell them: It isn't happiness that matters, only growth, cross-fertilization! As if they'd listen, as if they could hear at this point. They were in another world. She could only watch from the outside, and hope. Let them grow; let them help each other grow. Mark had growth in him. But Sally—

Frances looked at the bride under the mist of veiling. The delicate profile, the smooth polished cap of hair, not a strand out of place, so perfect. Almost too perfect, too nice. Such a good bringing-up. Everything had come easily to Sally: good looks, health, background, money. And now—Frances felt a little bitter about it—Mark.

Why should Sally make an effort to grow? Growth was uncomfortable. Wouldn't she just keep Mark in a nice comfortable copy of her mother's and father's marriage?

Well, what was the matter with it? Frances considered. Weren't the McNeils happy? There they were, standing securely side by side. They had a good marriage, sup-posedly, and attractive children, a lovely home, and their place in the community.

Wasn't this what one wanted?

They looked quite contented, settled back into their

positions after John's big moment in the service, giving away his daughter. Relieved and satisfied, they looked, as if everything were in hand now. What was wrong with that?

The image flashed into Frances's mind of those espaliered fruit trees in France, trained against a southern wall, protected and bountiful but not full round trees; all flattened out to one dimension, deformed to fit a wall, to produce fruit. No, not what one wanted; not her idea of a good marriage.

Wasn't it possible, a good marriage? They all wanted it, for themselves, for Mark and Sally, for each new couple at the altar. But to whom could she point?

Frances looked around at the lifted faces, so open now, laid bare to the music that was interrupting the service. Everyone seemed alone in his dream, like her.

Her glance turned to Beatrice and Spencer standing together, stopped short, and rested on them. Yes, these two—Frances looked at her old friends—they had it all: a good marriage, harmony and growth, a last growth they could share.

But even so, was it perfect? Beatrice and Spencer, too, Frances thought, looked at the bride and groom with some heartbreak. Did she imagine it? After all, Mark and Sally weren't *their* children.

Their children? Of course not, they had no children. Spencer had none; Beatrice, only one, by another man. Marriage wasn't complete for them either—no fruit.

This was what she wanted for Mark, for Mark and Sally: fruit and flowers, leaves and roots, the whole tree. What Beatrice and Spencer didn't have, or John and Deborah, or she herself—she and Stephen.

All you had missed, yourself, you wanted to give your children. But you never could, only in the externals, sometimes: a summer by the sea, a college education. But it wasn't enough. You wanted to give courage, wisdom, happiness. Was it never possible to give the real things? Not happiness, perhaps, but at least some awareness, to keep them from stumbling blindly as she had done.

A little insight—if only she'd had it earlier! But some people never got it at all. Or so late—Beatrice and Spencer—through experience and suffering.

Would Mark have to go through mistakes and heartbreak—unhappiness, even, in this marriage—to find out about life and himself? Could she bear to watch him go through her experience, wait for better luck next time? A second marriage, was this her best hope for him? What a thought for a mother to have at her son's wedding.

Could nothing be learned or handed on to your children? Wisdom seemed to be acquired only through suffering and carried with pain, like Isaiah's "burden of the valley of vision." For her it had been like this; but some people were able to carry wisdom, even to share it, with more grace.

Deborah's father, for instance, over there. Frances wondered about the old man standing across the aisle next to his daughter. She knew he had suffered—there was the older daughter who died, and now his wife—but his face had a serenity she envied. Not the fake peace of the old-fashioned world of her mother, a cheap acceptance, bought by wearing blinders, by cutting yourself off from life around you. Whatever Theodore had—wisdom, serenity, understanding, she couldn't define it exactly—he was able to communicate to others, even to her.

Perhaps illumination could be passed on sometimes. There was a possibility, a crack of light here. She had been near it before, had almost reached it last night, had fallen asleep on the fringe of comfort. But what it was she couldn't remember. No time to find out now. She must pull herself back to the service; she must be ready to meet people, to talk, to laugh, to say good-by.

". . . *that ye may so live together in this life, that in the world to come ye may have life everlasting.*"

Life everlasting, a hollow phrase. Who wanted *that*? *Light* everlasting, perhaps she had misheard the minister. Life or light? Light or life?

Theodore

"O Lord our God, under the shadow of Thy wings let us hope . . ."

Theodore felt the great weight of years fall from him, borne aloft on the wings of St. Augustine's prayer. A favorite of his, he had persuaded Sally to put it in the service. His beloved grandchild Sally, a bride today, leaving them. It was a last gift from her, this prayer. He could not see her face now, her head bent under the veil, but she was thinking of him. They had a bond, grandfather and grandchild, a direct bond that bypassed parents. Sally was not really like her mother, Deborah; less tentative, more positive, like Suzannah, he preferred to think, as he first knew his wife. There was a kind of dash to her. She reminded him of a frisky pony sometimes, with that blonde mane. A bit of the rebel in her—like Suzannah there, too. A mind of her own, but ready to touch you with a quick act of closeness, like this.

". . . under the shadow of Thy wings let us hope . . ."

Magnificent first line, like a great bird taking flight, swept aloft on the hope, the belief in God. A great gust of hope—a great gust of a prayer.

Not all prayers lifted you so immediately into the presence of God. But this one—not a prayer actually, a paragraph from *The Confessions*—this one was a desperate cry of hunger from a human heart. With a single leap it spanned the distance between man and God, and the distance between man and man, too.

". . . *Thou wilt support us, both when little, and even to gray hairs. . . .*"

It embraced all the stumbling stages of his own long life, Theodore felt, and the many different stages of life in this room. All his friends and family gathered here together, it embraced, no matter where they were in years or experience: Sally and her young man, expectant at the altar; Deborah and John, in those distracted middle years; Henrietta and Don, in some separate and unhappy state; Harriet in the set resignation of the old; and even the grandchildren, those bright shoots of life, springing up bold and unaware—this great wing covered them all.

". . . *When our strength is of Thee, it is strength . . .*"

The prayer had gained its height now and sailed along at a sustained level, in the serene upper atmosphere.

". . . *but, when our own, it is feebleness. . . .*"

This was what he believed in life; the central core of his belief, his conception of a stream of compassion which fed the world. When it flowed through us, all action was furthered along, was pure and good, was "strength." But outside of it, our efforts were against the tide; puny, only half effective.

The arid periods of his life, now he looked back at them, were when he had been forced, by sheer busyness and distraction, to work outside the stream—the arid middle years, the years of success in the world. Would it have been different if he had been a professor like his father, instead of a lawyer and banker? His father was never successful; probably that was why he, himself, had to be—why he chose that road.

It wasn't the profession, though, that kept you from the stream. Maybe it was just part of the middle years, where Deborah and John were now, bogged down by the busyness of life, too distracted to listen.

It wasn't their fault, really. He wasn't a puritan about life. The gaining of wealth wasn't in itself sinful; the world wasn't necessarily wicked. But these things kept you too busy, too bogged down, to find the stream. You simply couldn't hear it. There was no time to listen. In this sense it was true, the saying he had struggled over: it was harder for a rich man to enter the kingdom of heaven than for a camel to go through the needle's eye.

Was it a necessary stage, those fighting middle years? One had to forge ahead, like a healthy animal, aggressive and ambitious, learning one's own strength and just how far it went. After the dependence of youth, one had to gain self-reliance, self-confidence. The watchword of the middle years, self-confidence, and the watchword of modern civilization, too, its education and thinking. Psychology was always preaching self-confidence. A fine thing, too (Theodore attempted to be tolerant), as far as it went. But it only went halfway, he thought.

That was the trouble with psychiatry. Don, for instance, over there, his good son-in-law; he always enjoyed talking with Don on the common grounds of psychiatry and religion—the emphasis on being rather than doing; inward looking, rather than outward acting, human values rather than mechanical ones. Good, all this. Not particularly original, of course—they always acted as though they'd discovered the inner life, these bright young men—but good and true.

Self-awareness as a guide to balanced living was sound, he felt, by whatever road you took. "Know thyself": the Orientals, the Greeks, the Hebrews had preached the same thing, in one form or another. It was no invention of psychiatry; but after all, truth had to come back in new forms, under new names. He didn't begrudge them the names, or the credit. Though he sometimes wished they'd have a little humility. Even a little humor would help. But then, no new sect ever had humor; no disciples either, even the disciples of Christ.

It took time; it took age to ripen humor, and these people were so young and earnest. He didn't quarrel with them. He could see a race of young people growing up much more aware of their motives and desires, much more honest toward themselves and others, conscientiously trying to follow the inner law of their lives, toward a new integrity, as Don said. A good aim—he couldn't quarrel with it—but still in the making; only half worked out, it seemed to him.

What this generation attempted, poor children, was a most difficult technique of living totally aware every moment, rather like walking a tightrope at the top of a circus tent. No handrails up there. They'd abandoned the conventional rules. Every step had to be a disciplined act of skill. One false move, and down to the sawdust they went. Not even a safety net to soften the fall.

In religion, there was always the safety net of God's love—not that the tightrope was any easier to walk. "Be ye therefore perfect" was just as much of a knife edge, just as hard to balance on, as the new tightrope of self-awareness. But there was always that net of God's love to save you.

What was there in psychiatry? Self-respect? Self-love? Human love? That's what Don argued.

But true compassion, the only kind of love that helped, wasn't this pretty close to God's love, if not the same thing? In the end, it led right back to God.

"*. . . We return unto Thee, O Lord . . .*"

Mankind kept returning, and finding the same thing in other terms; it was the direction that mattered.

"*. . . our souls may rise toward Thee . . .*"

Consciously or unconsciously, the direction was constant.

"*. . . leaning on the things which Thou hast created . . .*"

Ah, *this* was the phrase that pointed the way, Theodore felt, that contained the secret of human life. "Leaning on the things which Thou hast created, and passing on to Thyself, who hast wonderfully made them." To bridge the human and the divine—this was what we were here in life to do. Human love became a bridge to God. All human loves led to God, otherwise they were barren.

But you had to start with human love—where Sally and Mark were now, "leaning on the things which Thou hast created." From the physical to the spiritual: that was marriage, the history of all marriage, his own and every good one. "He should begin by loving earthly things." Plato was right—"From fair forms to fair conduct." One should never lose sight of the fair forms, though. He was certain of that. As long as we were on earth we were human creatures. "Creatureliness" was a blessing; he was grateful for it—all the creaturely beauty he had known.

How beautiful Suzannah had been when he first met her at that skating party. She wore a bright plaid skirt, long to the ground. He didn't know how they ever skated in those garments—very different from Sally's ski trousers. Suzannah had looked quite dashing just the same, a tam-o'shanter tilted on her head. She sparkled that evening. A kind of fire burned in her; he had been caught by it. It had burned in her all her life, and was burning in Sally now.

How clumsy he had been, to her quick flamelike quality. She seemed utterly unattainable to him, poor professor's son, stolid Pennsylvania Dutch. Impossible that he should win her. But he went after her as he went after his degree in college, or his career later. He was determined to win her, and he did; he did. When she finally yielded, it was worth all the effort.

Oh, he had everything, he realized; he regretted none of it. Even that incident on their honeymoon, when he took her bridal nightgown and burned it up in the stove, in the Maine woods cabin. How he shocked his Suzannah.

He still felt rather shamefaced about it. His violence had shocked her, his passion, perhaps—but chiefly, his *waste*. Her puritan thrift was terribly affronted by his romantic gesture—the beautiful batiste gown, made by Aunt Matilda, all the work on it, so dainty with the long-cuffed sleeves, just as fine as one could buy abroad.

Besides, it smelled in the stove, an acrid smell of cloth burning. Suzannah laughed, in spite of her disapproval, and told him he was being punished for his wickedness. It wasn't wickedness, he said, only ardor inspired by her beauty. Anyway it was a delicious smell, he insisted, the smell of burning cloth. How they had laughed together. Wonderful laughter, the joy of reunion after a first separation. It was always a little joke between them: "the delicious smell of burning cloth."

A joke he couldn't share any more—such a trivial thing to regret. But it was the trivial things you regretted. You came to terms with the big things. They were still intact, even shared in some way; only the little things vanished. He couldn't help grieving over them a bit; the little things were what made life wonderful. They were holy, too; part of the miracle of *the Word made flesh*.

Marriage itself was the Word made flesh, according to him. It was an expression of the divine in the creature; a manifestation of the spirit in the flesh; a tangible symbol of the great truth we were here on earth to learn and to live: to be a vessel for that Word. For it always seemed to Theodore that the Word made flesh was not only Christ's coming down to earth, but the creation of earth itself and each creation on earth, each child and each work of art. Even Albert—not that he knew or cared—participated in the Word made flesh.

But a child was the truest expression. Marriage could hardly be expressed without it. Love must be made visible. The sin of immorality, he sometimes felt—though he could hardly say this to the young—was not that it went too far, but that it didn't go far enough.

If you really loved a man, judging from Suzannah, you wanted to bear his child. If you really loved a woman, you wanted her to bear your child. The meaning and expression of love wasn't complete until you looked at your firstborn.

His first look at Agnes—he would never forget it. Or rather, their first look at her together; his first look was too distraught. He was only thinking about Suzannah and hardly saw the baby, that bundle of blankets the nurse brought out of his wife's room. That wizened little thing with the misshaped head—Suzannah had suffered for this? Hours and hours, outside the closed door of their bedroom, he heard her strange moaning breaths, like an animal in pain. So inhuman, it sounded. Had Suzannah been hideously transformed—like their once familiar room, now alien with the smell of disinfectants? If only she would scream, he thought, it would be more human, more natural. She was always so brave, so self-controlled.

At last he was allowed into the room. (How locked out of this female rite fathers were in his day. How insignificant, even guilty, they were made to feel.) Suzannah, with her hair brushed strangely smooth, was lying in an unfamiliar hospital-neat bed, rather wan but quite serene, smiling at him. The baby lay in the laundry basket Suzannah had fixed for her, less red now, and asleep. Suzannah was immediately herself, full of practical details. "You see, she fits perfectly in the basket. Doesn't she look sweet?"

He couldn't say anything; Suzannah went on and on. "The nurse says her head won't be so lopsided after a week or two." She was full of ideas. "Now we really have to decide what to name her."

But he—he couldn't leap into ordinary life so quickly. He couldn't do anything, he remembered, except hold Suzannah's hand and look at this new, close-lidded life— the union of Suzannah's and his. No mistaking that. Suzannah's tip-tilted nose and his own mother's mouth, curiously reproduced in miniature in this tiny creature who would outlive them and go on into the future, a living testimony to their love.

How could they have known she would *not* outlive them? She lived only twenty-five years, and died in the bloom of womanhood—the tragedy of their lives. He hadn't felt the same way about the other two babies when they came along. He hadn't stopped to think, looking at Deborah and Henrietta, that they would outlive him; he just took it as a matter of course. Only with Agnes, their first-born—Agnes, who died.

He loved the other two, naturally; but Agnes was something incredible—their golden first-born, a golden child, a golden woman. Suzannah never recovered from her loss. If only he could have spared her this! She had never accepted it, never forgave God for taking Agnes, for cutting off that bright future. She could not make the loss a part of the fabric of her life. It was always an excrescence, an unassimilated burden to be carried daily, yearly, and sacrificially. Suzannah was a rebel till the end.

This grief, Theodore realized, was one of the few separating things in their life together. He couldn't help Suzannah here; he couldn't reach her. This particular part of her had died. If she had wept and grieved, he could have comforted her; the ground would have bloomed again. But it was a sealed-over area no one could reach, where nothing would ever grow.

He had learned then about the isolation of grief, even for those in the same grief. Grief can't be shared. Everyone carries it alone, his own burden, his own way.

He had grieved too, in a different way, but he had gradually accepted the loss, absorbed it somehow into his being. Finally he was able to return the flesh to spirit.

This, too, one had to learn, Theodore discovered. The flesh must be made Word. St. Augustine knew; he too had lost his first-born, his son. He understood loss and accepted it, the only way one could; otherwise he would never have written those lines. "For he only loses none dear to him, to whom all are dear, in Him who cannot be lost." There it was, the lesson of the flesh made Word, the consecration of the act.

All human acts, Theodore felt now, were meant to be consecrated to God. Not in pain, as he had done, but naturally and joyfully as a rule of life, like the monks and the nuns consecrating every act and incident of the day. Even among common people in the older civilizations, there were traces of it; in those Gaelic prayers, for instance, not only for meat and drink but for laying the fire and work in the fields. This sense of consecration, where had it gone? Marriage had it still, one of the few acts—its frame, its form, its very words—openly dedicated to God.

". . . O God, who has so consecrated the state of Matrimony that in it is represented the spiritual marriage . . . Look mercifully upon these thy servants . . ."

Look mercifully, yes, upon these children—upon all his children here in this room—even if they did not understand. How could he expect his children to understand the consecrated act, when he had only understood at the end of his life?

It was death, really, Suzannah's dying, that had taught him dedication. All things done for her during her long invalidism, this period of unconscious withdrawal from life, were illumined with love. To wash, to lift, to smooth, to change a position, to feed—the humblest details became beautiful.

Beautiful—strange word; meaningful, perhaps. All had meaning and purpose, because of love. He understood the incredible phrase: "All that is, is holy," and Brother Lawrence, dedicating to God the most menial work in the monastery, the washing of pots and pans.

Women, doctors, and nurses, Theodore realized, practice dedication in their ordinary work. Women learn it naturally with their babies. Suzannah had learned it with Agnes; expressed it with her hands and her body, never in words. But now, looking back, he could see that what he was learning late through his intense life of service for her, she had known and lived instinctively long before.

Even in the nine months of bearing a child, this was Suzannah's secret serenity. Everything was for the child; the sun on her hand, the food she ate, the sleep on her pillow. All common living had meaning and beauty, because it went to the child growing in her. And when the babies were small, her intense delight with the homely details. How he had laughed at her, running down the stairs with a dirty diaper, exclaiming, "What a beautiful stool!" And all those rites: the purification of the morning bath, the sacrament of orange juice, the ritual of the good-night glass of water—he understood them now. As usual, Suzannah had been ahead of him. He had followed her haltingly, caught up with her at last, in the stumbling solemn way he always had to learn.

But now they had reached the same point. They were together in their love and understanding of love. This belief sustained him. The children wondered how he could bear her last illness. They could not understand the nature of their love—their great love which had carried them along, in which they were still immersed. Such love, once experienced, has the nature of something eternal. His children wasted their sympathy on him. He had received what life had to offer; the reality was so great he could not feel it damaged, even now.

Now? he asked himself. Why, *now*, at the end of his life, a new dimension existed: the communication of love itself in service; wordless, nameless, and all-pervading; transfiguring his daily life. And this experience—it astonished him—was the best of all.

How strange it was, and how little they would believe him—his near and dear ones in this room—if he should tell them. If he should say at a wedding, the apex of love's expression, that the richest experience of loving had come to him at the end of his life. Like the miracle of Cana, Christ's first miracle—at a wedding, too—the wonderful remark of the steward: "Thou hast kept the good wine until now." For him it was true.

They wouldn't believe him, Theodore realized, looking around at the peacefully unconscious faces in the room. They wouldn't listen; they were as closed to him and his thoughts as children in a first sleep, dreaming their own light dreams. Or perhaps he was in a dream of his own, and they were awake to reality. For the life of him, he couldn't say which was the dream world and which the real. Only there was no bridge between the two. His children couldn't understand.

Someday they might, he tried to persuade himself. No, they couldn't understand because they hadn't had this experience of great love, of truly happy marriage. It grieved him, but he had to admit it to himself; he had never said it to Suzannah. He didn't think it was imagination or the difference between the generations; neither Deborah nor Henrietta was happy, as he and Suzannah had been.

What happened to them? They had married fine upstanding men; he liked both his sons-in-law. It seemed to be in the girls themselves. Some essential was lacking. Did he and Suzannah not give them the proper example of marriage? Their own great all-absorbing happiness— did it shut out the children? Where had they failed?

Deborah might be all right. He glanced at his daughter next to him, shifting back and forth on her feet, tired from the long stand and the day's excitement. Her face was wistful, as usual, as though she were looking for something. Would she ever find it?

And Henrietta? Theodore caught a glimpse of her hurt-child's face, turned away from Don's. But was it the fault of the marriage? Even as a girl she always had that expression, as if something had been taken from her, or were about to be taken. She had everything exactly like the others. They wanted a boy, of course—their third girl—but it didn't matter after the first week. Henrietta, they called her, after Suzannah's father, Henry, the name they planned for the boy.

But she was never a very happy child, and wasn't happy now. He was glad Suzannah had not noticed it or had refused to notice it. No, neither of his daughters had found complete happiness.

But happiness wasn't anything you found, in marriage or in life, for that matter. You shouldn't look for it or expect it. Marriage, in his experience, wasn't primarily concerned with happiness. It was too intent on something else—love, he supposed; but not the kind young people sang about today. *Ti voglio bene*, the Italian phrase, was closer to the meaning: *I wish what is best for you*. If you wanted the best for the other person, everything else followed, happiness too.

Though happiness couldn't begin to cover what he and Suzannah shared: the slow, cumulative growth of ups and downs, sadness and joy, drudgery and fun, strange arid periods and surprising renewals, all building up to the indissoluble closeness where he was now.

But come to think of it (Theodore stopped himself and looked around), who in this room was old enough to have had such an experience? No one but he could attest to this kind of companionship, born of long years of sharing, that ran ahead of language until in the end it replaced language altogether. In the end, where he was now, language wasn't even necessary. How could the young understand?

His two girls—Theodore found his mind sliding off the

stony impasse of his children's unhappiness, seeking smoother bypaths—they were no different from most young married couples, a lot happier than some. Deborah and John were quite compatible, a fine family, too. Henrietta, after all, had those beautiful children.

But was this happiness in marriage? He was facing the same stony impasse. It wasn't what he and Suzannah had, no matter what you called it.

"*. . . that their home may be a haven of blessing and of peace . . .*"

Yes, blessing and peace he and Suzannah had in their home. That beautiful phrase in the service—was it an outmoded dream? Did the state of the world today make it impossible? With wars and total annihilation hanging over them, it was absurd to expect peace anywhere, probably, even in the intimacy of a home. Homes couldn't help reflecting the conflicts in the world.

In his day it was different, people kept saying. Maybe they were right. He might be just an old fogy living in a time gone by. A peaceful enough time, his youth; but how about his father and mother, or his grandparents? Wasn't there just as much to tear families apart during the Civil War? Or in the Thirty Years' War, for that matter, were individuals any happier or more secure? It was hard to tell about such intimate things. Even in his day, people didn't talk much about their feelings. Marriages like his and Suzannah's—how often did they happen? How many did he know, then or now?

Glancing over his shoulder involuntarily, his eyes caught sight of Beatrice and Spencer standing together.

Ah—*they* had it, he knew with a flash of recognition. He couldn't say why he was sure, or what convinced him. The couple themselves he had hardly seen. His brief glimpse was so quickly overlaid with a vision of Suzannah and himself as they had once been, and then Sally and Mark as they might be.

Theodore stiffened and looked straight ahead, focusing on the real bridal couple to clear his blurred vision.

That was the trouble with old age; you no longer saw things singly—always with fuzzy edges. He saw too much. And yet Beatrice and Spencer, Suzannah and himself: here happy marriage was a reality. It existed, even if not for Deborah or Henrietta.

Agnes, perhaps, had she lived (he comforted himself with the thought)—Agnes had such a wonderful start with that fine fellow. He went back to his home town after she died, poor boy. They had been married only a year, and no children. Without children, marriage, as he saw it, wasn't complete, never quite solidified. It was something else, a love affair, a liaison, rare and beautiful and close sometimes, but not exactly marriage. No, she had died too soon.

But had she lived—had she lived, he found himself questioning—wouldn't she have had the perfect marriage? A home that was a "haven of blessing and of peace"?

Even as he asked the question, Theodore knew he couldn't answer it. He didn't know, any more than he knew about the two at the window. It was a mystery. He only knew that happiness in marriage existed. He had experienced it.

But even for those who hadn't, who were looking at it

from the outside, surely happiness in marriage existed, if only as a dream. Deborah and John, Henrietta and Don, Albert, Harriet: they believed in a happy marriage, whether they'd been happy or not. Otherwise, why did people come to weddings? Why were they moved by the bride and groom? Why were they suddenly reduced to credulous children at the ceremony?

Theodore shifted his stand; the stony impasse disappeared, and he felt level ground beneath his feet again. Weddings, he said to himself, expressed the eternal hope of the human race. Even to agnostics and cynics, weddings had a special significance that he, for his part, could only call religious. For a wedding was not only a promise and a pledge made in the eye of God and man; it was a heightening of human life by the addition of something beyond it, something uncertain, intangible, impossible to prove. An assertion of man's belief in a quality of spirit— love.

"God the Father, God the Son, God the Holy Ghost, bless, preserve, and keep you; the Lord mercifully with his favour look upon you, and fill you with all spiritual benediction and grace; that ye may so live together in this life, that in the world to come ye may have life everlasting. Amen."

The Bride and Groom

It was over, then. The first few chords of the Mendelssohn march struck up with a flourish. Dance, dance, the notes rang out from the musicians' corner. The cocks crowed morning and the bells pealed resurrection. An end to the silence, the stillness, the thoughts stretched out to breaking point. The long, sweet attenuated movement of the ceremony itself broke into a many-stranded finale.

The couple at the window looked up and faced one another, smiling in a daze of surprised recognition. Waking as from a dream, the bride and groom rediscovered each other with relief, no longer the terrifying strangers they had seemed at the start of the service.

We, who were strangers, are now man and wife, familiar from time immemorial, familiar to the end of the world. We, who were asleep, are now awake, to a new world. We, who were frightened, are now strong and confident. We, who were caught in a pattern, are now free to be ourselves—for the first time. We, who were children, are now heirs to a new estate— Come!

They turned, arm in arm, and started back toward the room of waiting friends. Lightly, gaily, they started back, half lilting to the music. How different from the leaden dirge up the aisle toward a moment of solemnity, toward the passing of time, toward death and eternity. Now they were dancing back to life, life instantaneous, life overflowing, open-armed life.

It was over now for the mothers and fathers. They stood, a little crumpled (John and Deborah, Frances and Stephen), watching their children turn and face the other way. On the march up the aisle, encased in a frame of formality, they seemed to have more stature. Now, suddenly bereft of the form, they looked diminished. Back in their small vulnerable human frames, they felt older and tired, pushed across the threshold, left behind.

It was over, too, for the wedding guests. A rustle of eased tension stirred through the room. At last, it was over. What a relief. Heads turned; faces lifted; feet shuffled; bodies leaned forward; eyes met, recognized, greeted; smiles and nods were exchanged. No longer separate souls reliving their lives in solitary thought, they were friends, kinsmen, united by the bonds of a family wedding.

We, wedding guests, who have been alone, isolated in our prison cells, muffled in the cocoons of our thoughts, are now joined again, part of the human community. We, who have descended into the dim past, are risen from the dead. We, who have been disembodied spirits at the Day of Judgment, are now reborn, flesh and blood again with another chance.

Life was no longer a great moment, a pinnacle in time. One cannot stand on the pinnacle. One sees too much, becomes dizzy. Climb down; drop to the path at one's feet, eye on the next step only, on the next moment, a succession of ordinary moments. What a relief. Find your handkerchief; straighten your hat; wipe your forehead; loosen your collar and tie. Ordinary moments were easier, small interstices of time to fill with the comforting minutiae of life: powder your nose, hold a teacup, have a sandwich. Life had ceased to toll mortality; it was merely ticking the ordinary moments again.

The music played itself out, leaving behind a silence still pulsing to the old rhythm, not yet filled with the new clamor of human voices. In the momentary hush, the bride and groom stopped and faced the assembly, hesitating on their island of invulnerability, before they merged into the eager crowd of friends.

It is life we have waked to, blazed on the faces of the bride and groom—*life and love and happiness.* Arrogantly and triumphantly, it blazed.

The lines of guests fluttered uncertainly, swayed, and then turned in a mass toward the young couple, as to the sun, or an open door.

It is life we have waked to, returned the faces of the guests in pale reflection of the bride and groom. *Not mortality and might-have-beens. Those heavy thoughts that held us just now were bad dreams. It is life and love and happiness that are real. Look, it is still there, for the bride and groom—for us, too, perhaps. It is still there, while it lasts. Hurry, while it lasts. Hurry, let us touch it, taste it, drink it!*

The stiff rows rippled and broke into separate figures which juggled themselves this way and that, into a new pattern, and then fell, in a humming swarm, around the bride and groom.

The Supper

"A kiss for the bride—doesn't the groom get kissed, too?"

"Mark, my congratulations—take care of her now."

"Yes, sir, I—"

"We could hear you even on the landing, Mark."

"Do say a word to Sigrid, dear, she made all the sand-wiches."

"Just beautiful, Miss Sally— Oh, I mean, Mrs. Gal-latin—"

"What does it feel like, Sal, to be Mrs. Gallatin? *An-other* Mrs. Gallatin. There are three Mrs. Gallatins, now, aren't there? How funny!"

"You're holding up the procession, children. Come along, Sheila—let's get married! How about it? A waltz, anyway: *Love and marriage, love and marriage, go together like a horse and carriage—*"

"The champagne, Jake—get it started, will you? André will help. In the pantry, yes. And don't forget the sandwiches. Chrissie, my dear, go after him—"

"Thank you—thank you. Yes, aren't they a lovely couple—just lovely."

Deborah was shaking hands abstractedly, a permanent smile on her face. Overgracious, she realized, to cover up anxiety; the glazed smile to compensate for the wandering eye, scanning the room for signs of trouble or delay. Had the minister left yet? Such a shame they couldn't stay for supper. It would have prolonged the sense of ceremony, and given her support. All those good-bys, and saying something nice to everyone, nibbled away at her strength. She felt cut up into slices, thin smiling slices, sugary slices of pink watermelon. Why did you have to cut yourself up into watermelon slices to feed people, she wondered. Weren't there enough sandwiches and champagne to last them until supper?

Not everyone was staying for supper, just family and a few friends. Should she have asked everyone? No, there wasn't room at the table. But there were enough sandwiches and champagne. She had counted all the extra people and there was plenty. It seemed to be circulating well, too. Only one broken glass, as far as she could see, spilled on old Mrs. Gallatin's dress. Well, it was almost over. The outsiders were gradually thinning out; still one or two neighbors left straggling her way to say good-by.

"Thank you so much— Well, *we* think so, too, naturally. So happy you could come—"

Only the supper party left now—Deborah took stock swiftly—settling into groups. There was the bride's group, still knotty with young people and children. Then there was the seated group around the old lady on the sofa. Deborah was glad someone could sit down; her feet hurt.

How long till she could get all her guests into the dining room, peacefully eating? Then her responsibility would be over. Mostly, anyway. Sigrid was already making signals at the door. She must catch John's eye—or Father's —or Sal's? Yes, Sal and Mark must begin.

Then suddenly—she never knew quite how or why—the

room began to crystallize. Couples were moving toward the door, like sand through an hourglass. Sally and Mark first, slowly and rather self-consciously, Sal on Mark's arm. Everyone stopped to look at them.

How many times they would do this! Deborah felt the lump in her throat again. How many times, arm in arm, but this was the first. She would remember it; they would all remember it, she thought, as she turned to follow.

The supper was good, Deborah noted, relaxed in her seat. Her guests, now withdrawn from her, had turned to the business of eating. With relief, with intense gusto, they fell on the food—as if they had been out in the fields haying, Deborah thought, instead of simply standing around watching a ceremony.

There was something about big emotional moments; you always felt ravenous afterward. At concerts, too, she remembered—such an anticlimax, after that high spiritual plane. But it invariably happened, a swing of the pendulum, as though people were afraid to be too removed from earth and needed the reassurance of solid food.

She was pleased, at the moment, to have her guests relish the supper. It was delicious; the soup had just enough sherry; the steak was not overdone; the lettuce had been properly dried before the dressing went on—well mixed, not a drop of water.

All the hours of planning and preparation paid off at last. The guests around the table suddenly revived; their voices rose; their cheeks grew pink. How easily they seemed satisfied, like a bunch of children, glowing with nourishment. Deborah felt a deep satisfaction observing them. *I* have fed them, she thought; *I* have brought them life.

It was more than food, it seemed to her in this pleasant lull of dinner. Not only their faces and eyes glowed; they were coming to life inside. They looked relaxed, more themselves—the children, almost *too* much themselves. Should she have left them alone in that corner? They soared up like kites, sky-high and boisterous, tugging in all directions.

And the grownups' table—looking down its whole length to John at the other end—they had all come to themselves. Only a little *better* than themselves, Deborah thought. They were opening up, talking and getting on together, even those she had been most doubtful of. Aunt Harriet was listening to Albert; Spencer was drawing out Henrietta. Was it just the champagne? Or were people at their best at weddings?

Only the bride's table, she noticed, over Albert's shock of white hair, seemed the most reserved—oddly enough— on its best behavior. They were too conscious, perhaps, of being the center of all eyes, of having to live up to their important role. Or was it their age—too near adolescence to be sure who they were, still feeling safer in a formal pattern?

How long it took to learn who you were, Deborah sighed, to relax into it and accept it. Had she herself ever really—

"What are you thinking, my dear?" Albert leaned toward her benevolently. "You ought to be very happy."

"I was just thinking," she said in a burst of spontaneity, "how long it takes to learn to know oneself."

"Ah, *that* is something I have never learned," Albert said, unexpectedly humble.

"But in music, surely?"

"Oh, in music one is so much more than oneself. Or I might put it the other way round. One is so much less oneself, because the music is everything; it is all that matters; oneself doesn't matter at all. So you don't get to know yourself very well if you are an artist—a creative artist.

"Of course," he added, glancing across the table at his brother, "the would-be artists get to know themselves. At least they *try* hard enough, spend all their time looking at themselves, hardly see anything else."

At this point, the steak came between them again and Albert was absorbed.

The would-be artists. Deborah turned the phrase over in her mind. Yes, she was one of these. She had wanted to paint, or write, or play the piano. She had a vague picture of herself as an artist, a dream image she hankered after. Never more than a dream, though. While this, all this—she looked at the room spread out before her, as one might look at a painting, in color and light and shadow—how real it was! The plump roses in Mother's Waterford glass; the light from Father's old candlesticks, glinting on wineglasses and plate rims, on polished silver and sheen of cloth, reflected finally in moving eyes and lips.

Real? Almost superreal. The scene glowed with the extra vividness of a field illumined by the last rays of evening sun. Didn't this matter more to her—to have created this scene? Wasn't it rather a triumph to have brought it about—to have mixed with infinite care the separate parts, weighing this detail, discarding that one? The many disparate pieces were part of it; the cream of crab soup, the Waterford glass, the torn-up scraps of seating arrangements—all fitted like pieces of mosaic to make the perfect whole. She had composed the exact setting needed to melt the divergent personalities of her guests, to start them exchanging words, thoughts, feelings. Through her they were freed to be themselves—a little more than themselves.

For through her, Deborah realized, a fresh spark had come to birth—a bond, an understanding, a communication. This was a creative act, wasn't it—as much as the perfect performance of a Rachmaninoff prelude she had once struggled for? Even more, it was her special creation, for it couldn't have been done by anyone else. It was hers —her individual work of art.

Of this Deborah was sure. But there was something else in the picture she was struggling to understand—something in this present occasion, this particular vision, she must uncover. It held a meaning for her, a secret message. And she longed for this message tremulously; like standing in front of a painting in an art gallery, or sitting at a concert, or that night listening to Father talk about "the stream." If only she could wait patiently enough, she was convinced, the secret would be delivered to her.

Deborah glanced down the long expanse of white tablecloth, to her husband at the other end. Between the rows of relatives he looked distant and dwarfed, suddenly small and human as he had in the wedding march. Yet she saw him freshly, as she did occasionally, catching an unexpected glimpse of him in a roomful of guests, recognizing with a start of surprise the stranger she had married. How distinguished this man's face; how well chiseled. How worn, but—yes, *distinguished*—her husband, John.

He was holding up his end of the table too, she noticed with some amusement; listening attentively to old Mrs. Gallatin, watching to see that things were passed along, catching her eye now and then for approval. Was it possible he was trying to please *her*? She was so used to thinking of herself as the weaker partner, leaning on him, it came to her as a shock that he might sometimes lean on her. The shift in weight made her feel stronger, more of a person. She was carrying her load; they were carrying it together. An equal partnership she had not sensed before.

She felt the firm bond between them, and the relatives on either side held together by this bond: grandmother and grandfather, aunts and uncles, children and grand-children behind them; spanning the past and the future, all linked together through them—herself and John. She was aware for the first time of the unity of the family groups they linked.

The phrase "the community of marriage" came to her from the old-fashioned past. *Community* was what they had together. And perhaps this was the meaning of marriage, not the communication she was forever looking for. Community—communion—communication: the words might be closer than she knew. All this they had made, shared, held together—wasn't it a form of communica-tion? At the moment it seemed enough. It compensated for all the humdrum grocery-string length of days. It gave a meaning to her life.

Was this then "real life"—that real life she was always wondering about and looking for; life stripped to its naked core, for once clear and vivid, not embedded in a chaotic lava flow? The ore of life was suddenly visible, the thin vein of gold, not covered as it usually was, to be dug out with difficulty, but on the surface, exposed and gleaming.

She could see it—this essential nerve of life—recognize its infinite diversity, as she looked from one face to another down the table: in Father's deep serenity, in Aunt Harriet's sharpness, and in Frances's intensity; in the children's faces, shining with expectancy, and in Sally's incandescence across the flowers.

This slender strand of life was passing from one to another in richness and variety and beauty. She felt the miraculous continuity, renewing itself in the children; and now, further still, through Mark and Sally—all passing through her, fed by her, and she knew, to go on without her, as it was going on without her mother. But she, Deborah, as an individual, as a separate entity, had been part of it, taken from it, given to it, almost without knowing.

Where had she heard that before? In a book—in a dream—in a quotation? *Without knowing—effortlessly:* she fumbled for the familiar line, the fragment of a tune that eluded her.

Oh, it was Father, she remembered—and the stream. When you are in it, he had said, it feeds you and you give from it. Everything you do and give is the stream flowing through you. Could it be this? The stream of compassion, he called it, that feeds the world. Perhaps it was. Perhaps, she thought, happiness welling up in her with the surge of conviction. Yes, this was true; this was real. She had climbed another step, and she sensed it almost tangibly. She felt taller—or, no, maybe stronger—or freer, was it? It was one of those moments in life when you knew you had crossed a threshold and entered a new stage. The most trivial thing might tell you, but it was unmistakable like the click of a door opening; putting your hair up, or the kiss after dancing school, or being called Mrs. McNeil for the first time; and that morning in the hospital, "Yes, it's a girl." This moment, too, she felt, sitting up very straight in her chair—this was a coming of age.

She must remember! Oh, she must remember this moment, for she was at last, for an instant anyway, part of the stream.

The Toast

"We are gathered together at this most festive occasion . . ." Albert pushed back his chair and rose with his champagne glass in his hand.

Frances found it difficult to listen to him. She was still steeped in the wedding service, or that moment just after the service when she found herself standing in front of Mark, speechless; mother and son facing each other in silence. A long conversation of a look: *Darling, it's over— You did beautifully— It's wonderful— I know— Don't worry, we're all right— Good-by.*

And then the moment was over; brief, but real as a door flung open. Direct, sudden, irrefutable as lightning —that look on Mark's face, blazing with happiness, lucid with certainty. What did he see in the future? What did he understand of the past? More than she realized? What did that lightning look imply? It carried a conviction she could not deny, but could not put into words, at least not yet—not now—not with Albert making a speech.

". . . a perfect occasion, a perfect couple—perfect happiness . . ."

What a conception, Frances thought. Did Albert believe in it still, after the third try? Did any of them believe in it? Weren't they all thinking of themselves and what they had wanted of marriage (she and Deborah, Albert and Don); all of them regretting different things;

all of them hoping for different things (Aunt Harriet and Theodore, Beatrice and Pierre)? What were they actually toasting? Happy marriage, at least they could agree on that for the couple.

But the trouble was, Frances thought as she scanned the listening faces, when people talked about happy marriage what they really meant was perfect marriage. She no longer believed in perfect marriage, or perfect happiness for that matter. It was just a dream; better to face it early. Sentimentality only made it worse. People were always sentimental beforehand, mouthing platitudes like Albert's speech, or watching that scene a few minutes ago when Mark took Sally's arm and they paced dramatically in to supper.

What a show, that stately walk up the steps, Sally leaning on Mark's arm in a kind of mock wifely dependence—Victorian as an old print. Not marriage at all; just a picture-book pose. Never again would it be like that—walking in to dinner. Sally would be in the kitchen in blue jeans, with a baby strapped to a high chair and screaming for pablum. Did they give pablum any more? And the diapers would be chugging away in the washer— if they had one—and the hamburgers smoking on the stove. Sal would shout above the uproar, "Come and get it, darling!"

But the *darling* would still be there, Frances was reasonably sure. And what's more, Mark would be right there, too, in the turmoil, bathing a child or scrubbing a floor, or carrying in laundry. He had done it for her as a little boy, and he would do it for Sally. This generation might shout at one another but they were grubbing together at the tasks to be done. Marriage was like that most of the time, covered with the dust of dailiness. But let's not call it perfection, Frances said firmly to herself, as she rose to her feet with the general shuffling of chairs.

No, Sally and Mark were not a perfect pair, and they would not have perfect happiness. They would have all the imperfections everyone else had. And yet she raised her glass with the group of solemn guests around the table, toasting some undefined dream, sharing some general hope.

What was the common denominator of their feelings, she wondered, watching each face in turn. For they were united at this moment, despite their incongruities: Deborah with her eyes full of tears; Aunt Harriet, barely touching the rim to her lips; Theodore, gazing into the distance; Don staring moonily at her over his glass—she didn't want to get entangled there.

And now John, at her side; such an earnest, angular man. What was he feeling? She had no idea. Nothing but unleavened clay in his solid face. Thank God she wasn't married to *him*. Stephen, at least—

Did she really feel this warmly about her husband? Frances glanced at him across the table. The mask was down and he flashed back a swift look of understanding, gaiety, and affection.

Recognition leaped in her. Yes, Stephen might lead her a dance and drive her to despair, but he had perception, even though obscured most of the time. When it sparked, one illuminating sentence a week, one illuminating look, was enough to live by.

This was why, she realized with the certainty of touch, as she found her chair again, she would never leave him. These moments counterbalanced all the others—at least, on her scales. And you had to use your own scales in life to weigh the moments that counted. No one else could weigh them for you, or make you see them differently; not even a friend like Beatrice. "You don't see life as it really is," Beatrice was always saying, "or Stephen as he is."

Was it a false picture, Frances asked herself, the image she saw and held up to Stephen? Relationship is a mirror, she read once, held up for the other person to see himself. But did the mirror reflect a photographic image? Wasn't it more of a portrait, with all the possibilities opening up behind, as in those Italian Renaissance paintings? What you saw for the other person was the hill, the tree, the winding road he might still take, the mountain in the distance he might scale, the shining port from which even now the boat unrolled its sail to catch a freshening wind.

But how could you see these vistas and not be disappointed if they never became realities? When the picture didn't come true, you felt tricked by your vision. Was the moment of vision an illusion that could never be lived by?

The moment of the toast they had just experienced— was it unreal? All those faces around the table, believing in something; all those bravely voiced hopes—were they false?

They couldn't be, Frances found herself protesting. In spite of Albert's speech, and the stage entrance of the bride and groom, and the tears in Deborah's eyes, the moment of the toast itself was real. There was an element here that wasn't an illusion, a core of reality her cynicism couldn't crack, a focus of intensity that fused a roomful of guests.

It was, she thought, groping for its essence, as though a seed of perfection existed at the heart of all the imperfections, and this moment was its expression: the moment of the toast, the moment of met glances, of shared hopes—the moment of a wedding itself.

And the bride and groom—Frances looked at them now in a new light. The bride and groom were its embodiment. They weren't posing any more; they were bending over the wedding cake, Mark holding Sally's hand to steady it. Their happiness at the core permeated the atmosphere, radiated through the company, filled up the cracks and mended the tears in the fabric of society. Their love at this moment overflowed a roomful of guests, like a high tide, covering rocks and crannies, floating limp seaweed, bringing all to life again. In such a medium, Frances felt, one could move without effort, as if suddenly immersed in the proper medium for human relations, the medium for life itself. Borne along by such a tide, one should ask nothing more, not even, as she was always doing, that it last.

Was it partly this, she wondered—because one knew the moment couldn't last, one relaxed in its fleetingness? One touched people in a unity of feeling—a single tide swept them all—but lightly; sharing, greeting, passing, demanding nothing.

She was always demanding too much of people and occasions. She met them with too much expectation, pursued them for perfection, and then, inevitably, was disillusioned.

Hadn't she done it all her life? Who was she to smile at Albert's toast and Deborah's tears? She, too, still clung to the dream of perfection. She had expected it with

Stephen, and failed; looked for it with a lover, and been disappointed. And now, a last chance, she wanted perfection for her son.

The vision of perfection, she faced it here again. The vistas of possibilities—must one reject them? Was it wrong to believe in them?

In the crystal lens of this moment, she felt she could test her deepest feelings, question true or false in herself and her life and find at last the answer. No, she knew with certainty, the possibilities were there and it was right to see them. Her mistake lay somewhere else, perhaps in the demanding. One had to perceive the possibilities in people, but not demand them. One had to believe, but not expect; see, but not clutch. What a razor edge for her to walk—she, who always wanted to force things by will power.

She would have to learn that she couldn't make the picture true for Stephen, or for Mark—hadn't she seen this watching Stephen paint?—because nothing creative came this way. A work of art couldn't be made true by sleight-of-hand or determination. It had to grow true; and growing—had she forgotten?—changed things. The fruit grew from the flower; the work of art, from the vision; the child, from the moment of ecstasy. You couldn't foresee just how it would grow or what form it would take; you couldn't cling to your vision, ask it to come in any particular way, or to last in any special form. Lasting killed things, the moment told her; letting go freed them to eternal life—in another form.

She could not give Mark happiness. Even last night she had sensed it. She would have to let him find it for himself in his own way. You could only give your children clues: a thread of perception, a crack of light, a key to a locked door. Parents, after all, were just doorkeepers. You might open a door for them that had been locked for you. Was this what she saw in Mark's glance? This much you could do for the other person: with honesty, with perception, you might open a door you had never been through yourself; point out a way you hadn't found soon enough to follow in your own life.

Ah—here was the place she reached last night; the clearing in the thicket, the illuminated meadow where she could stop and rest and sleep. Because of this opening, this crack of light, the terrible human chain of mistakes could be broken.

Mark need not have a marriage like hers—at last she understood his look—Mark was not Stephen; Sally was not Deborah. They would make their own future.

But now she must let go. They must all let go of this dream couple. Leave them to create their own reality, freshly, unimpeded by other people's hopes and fears. Only then would there be any possibility of a creative act.

Any possibility—and here, she realized for the first time, was the true meaning of the moment they were witnessing. The seed of perfection she had glimpsed—it was simply this: the possibility of a creative act. It was the seed they were toasting, nothing more. Their toast was a recognition of the possibility, but also an acknowledgment that it was not theirs to fulfill. Someone else would fulfill it. What the bride and groom made of it in the future was their responsibility; would be their discovery, a secret harvest the wedding guests might never see. But this moment could be seen. It was valid, as a closed seed is valid. It was the seed they believed in and were toasting; and it was the seed they were setting free. For the toast was both recognition and renunciation, both a greeting and a farewell. In this sense, it was essentially an act of faith. And it was the act of faith that fused them and made them one.

For they were united at this moment, Frances felt, looking around the table from face to glowing face. They were like brothers in a monastery, or early Christians, witnessing a miracle. "All one body, *we*," echoed in her, from an old Sunday-school hymn. "One in faith, and one in hope, and one in charit*ee*."

Yes, she loved them all at this moment: her husband and her son; her mother-in-law and her new daughter. There was no holding back, and no reaching forward. She had no enemies, and all her sins were forgiven. Dearly beloved—yes, it was true—they were gathered together. And for this purpose, surely: to attest to the validity of the seed. Not continuity or fulfillment, or even renewal, which parents clutch for, but something else, nameless, new, unknown, eternal.

"For ever and ever"? The familiar phrases of the wedding service still rang in her ears. "From this day forward." The words had no meaning—or perhaps, she thought, they now had meaning for the first time. But she could only stumble on new words, pricking up like fresh spears of grass through last year's dried stalks and leaves. Here—now—living—true: this is the life everlasting.

After

"Here they come!" someone shouted.

The little group around the bottom of the stairs, waiting for the bride and groom, surged up the steps to catch a first glimpse. Children, climbing the stair well, clung to the banisters.

The older people, taking coffee in the living room after supper, stopped talking and turned somewhat apprehensively toward the hall.

Why, it seems to me they just left the table, thought Deborah with dismay. Can they be going already? Sally never dressed so fast in her life before. For Mark, of course—

A slammed door, a clatter of feet down the hall. Sally stood on the top landing in her blue suit, with the bouquet in her hand. She leaned down for a moment toward the outstretched arms and upturned faces.

"There it goes!"

A scuffle of children and a few cries.

"That's not fair—she threw it right at Chrissie!"

"You'll be the next to go, Chrissie," Jake shouted magnanimously. "You'll be the next."

No, thought Aunt Harriet from her corner in the hall, I'll be the next to go—but they don't realize it.

A swift bolt down the stairs, through rice and confetti. Sally had her collar turned up and her hands over her hair.

"Oh, *really*, Jake!"

"Come on, Sal." Mark took her firmly by the arm. "Let's get going."

Mark! thought Frances as they swept by her. How anxious he was to go—not a look in her direction to say good-by—not a look! But after all, she had had her look, and it was enough. He must go; he was all right; he didn't need her. There were others—her husband, her daughter. She glanced at Phyllis in the crowd following the bride and groom.

They were out in the court, now, with children running pell-mell behind them.

"Say good-by to *me*! Say good-by to me, *too*."

In the confused medley of noise, a few significant sounds: the sharp slam of a door; the explosion of an engine; the spattering of gravel as the car started off.

"Good-by, good-by!" Dim calls in the distance. Headlights blazed, then blacked out around the corner.

The crowd of older people stood motionless in the hall where they had been left, facing the open door and the empty night. Silent, for once, waiting for life to ebb back.

At last, a leisurely shuffle of feet on gravel, a few wisps of conversation—the young drifted in, casually unconcerned.

"They sure made a quick getaway. Who put the bags in?"

The big door slammed on the night outside and the sudden collapsed silence inside.

"Oh, *Mother*!" cried Susie, throwing her arms around

Deborah's neck, "oh, Mother, I don't want them to go—I don't *want* them to go!" She burst into tears.

"I know, darling," said Deborah, "I know."

Why did life go roaring on and on just when you thought you had it fixed in a frame and could look at it? Her moment of illumination at the supper table was over. She was very tired and her feet hurt—and Sally had gone. She wished they would all go home and she would be left with John.

People were moving now, little lingering groups shifting slowly toward the door. It was breaking up, almost over. This was easier; there was something to do. As long as there was something to do, you didn't have to think or feel. But after they left—

"Good-by, yes—it *was* a lovely wedding, wasn't it? Well, thank you. We are *so* happy about him— Yes, I'm sure *they* will be, too."

Now, what was it—something she was going to do? Something she wanted to touch, to put her hand on. The next step, the next little step. A steppingstone—that was all. What was it?

Deborah looked around like a child, for a sign, a place, or a hand.

"John," she said, turning to her husband with sudden relief—"oh, John!"